Thank you to every person I have met in my life.
To each of you, I am grateful for all who you are, and all that you have shown me.

Published in 2025
Copyright © Karen Houston
Creator: Karen Houston
Title: Let Your Soul Breathe: Open your heart to you.

ISBN: 978-0-646-71494-3

 A catalogue record for this book is available from the National Library of Australia

Book layout and design by Peter Gamble, Canberra
Set in Helvetica Neue-Thin, 12/14, and MinervaModern.

This book or any portion thereof may not be reproduced or used in any manner whatsoever without the express written permission of the publisher.

Website: knowyourmagnificence.com

Let Your Soul Breathe
Open Your Heart To You.

Karen Houston

This book is dedicated to all living souls on this planet.

For those who are willing to take responsibility of them self and ask;

    'Who Am I?'

We come with nothing, we leave with nothing, nothing belongs to us, we only belong to ourselves.

Everyone has a life and everyone has a story.

Everyone has a choice, to follow their heart or their head.

My Mission is for Everyone:
To be happy, healthy & wealthy.
To feel energized and fulfilled in all that you do.
To love yourself for all who you are.
To instill positive energy in all whom you meet, and.
To make a difference everyday.

As we beat our own drum to the rhythm of our soul.
We can then beat our soul to the rhythm of mother earth.

Table of Contents

Preface	ix
Who I am	xiii
Prologue	xv
Who are we?	1
Are you standing strong in your foundation of love?	5
Or crumbling in your abandonment of you?	5
Our Journey	7
Change	13
Breathe	21
We Choose our own Lessons	27
Who Are You?	33
Why do we get sick?	41
How psychological issues manifest in our life	49
Let Go	55
Life Is Like a Jigsaw	59
Things to Ponder	63
Responsibility	65
Cleansing	71
From my Blogs	73
Healing Practices and Techniques	105
Chakras	111
Case Studies	151
About The Author	157
Source references	163

Preface

Let Your Soul Breathe, has been written for you to have an understanding of you. To bring you to an awareness physically and emotionally, that you are more that what you see. To open you up to your emotional aspect. To feel you.

No, two people's lives are the same. We all have had different experiences, some wonderful and amazing, some tragic and horrific. We all have different challenges to face in our daily lives, some great, some small. Regardless of what has happened, or is happening in our life, we all have hopes and dreams, and want to find a sense of peace, a sense of belonging, a sense of purpose, and to feel fulfilled.

We are all living in the process of our lives, on a timeless journey. It is not a race, there is no finish line. It is a quest, both on a conscious and subconscious level, to connect to our non-physical aspect, our emotional self. To feel that our self is worthy, whole and complete.

No one comes unscathed, we all come wounded. No one is devoid of this.

We all spend our lives achieving, proving, justifying, doing.

What we have to do is remember how to be our love to our self at every moment.

To know how to feel ok in our own skin and to know we are pure love.

To remember.

We have seven main chakras; there are seven days in a week; there are seven colours of the rainbow.

There is a seven-step system at the end of the book, giving you a seven-step process, to guide to the seven parts of your self and the seven colours of the rainbow.

This will assist you how to visualize and focus on, day by day. To learn how breathe work and chakra meditation can enhance your life, increasing your sense of wellbeing and effectiveness in this world.

This simple course will give you meaningful insights, as well as easy to understand practical tools, that you can incorporate easily into your daily life. You will learn to use colour visualization, affirmations and your breath as effective tools, experiencing their soothing effect on your mind, body and soul. It will teach you how to create a space of peace for yourself, wherever you are.

The course is flexible and adaptable, to be taken step by step, at a pace that works for you. It only takes a few minutes each day. If you skip a day or two, don't stress. This is about you allowing and feeling your power within.

Allow yourself to digest and feel your way through this book.

Pick up the book, put it down, let yourself process you, write what you feel. Breathe. There are no short cuts, so take your time. The journey of self has no beginning, and has no end. It is about having respect of yourself. Let yourself flow in your life and remember how to feel. How to just be and how to be your love to you.

You may wish to consider writing daily in a journal. As you write, you acknowledge, you feel, you allow. Make time for you. Listen to your 'self'. It wants you to prosper.

Enjoy!

Karen

Who I am

Before you begin to read *Let Your Soul Breathe*, I would like you to know and understand.

I do not call myself anything other than me, Karen. I am also known as Pixie.

I am not a spiritual guru or have any special powers.

I have a *knowing*, I listen, I process, I release.

I am human, just like every one of you.

I just trust and know if I can look past what is happening on a physical level, I can get the message that is being shown to me.

I am not cured, nor am I perfect. I process things every day.

I am just me living my journey and want you to know that we are all on our journeys. This means something different for every one of us.

All we need to know is that we are responsible for ourselves and no one else. Each and every one of our journeys is unique and ours to live.

I believe we are all born with a *knowing*, some remember, some don't.

We are born pure and we are born innocent and we are born of love.

I talk about, *we*, throughout the book, as we are all wounded, we are all energy and we are all dealing with our lives every day.

I do not claim to be any different from anyone, and I certainly do not mean to offend or cause upset to anyone who reads my book.

I am not a healer and I cannot heal anyone, or replace a medical professional.

We are all healers to our self. I can bring aspects of your self to your awareness.

This has been written to bring us to an understanding that we are energy and how we choose to process this, is up to each one of us.

We can all stop looking outside ourselves, and appreciate all that we are.

Nothing will change, until we make the change, or want to.

Sometimes, just to be accepted by another, stops us from following our journey to its full potential.

This is a story about my journey and hopefully along the way it will trigger something within you, a memory, a feeling, a *knowing*, to remember you.

Prologue

Ever since I can remember, I have always had a *knowing*, a *connection* to a higher energy.

As a young girl, I would often lie in my bed at night and feel that my head was the size of the room and my mouth was small like a bird. It was a strange but familiar sensation and I felt connected to all things.

As a young girl, I would also often sit at my dressing table at night, and look out at the moon and the stars and feel a real connection to a higher dimension, the whole universe.

Growing up, I felt indifferent and could not understand, why others could not relate to what I said, or how I felt, often being dismissed and misunderstood.

With my *knowing* and my *connection*, I know that we are not just born to live and then die. We are all connected to each one of us and each part of the universe. We all have a higher purpose, to remember our love in who we are in human form.

We are much more than what we see. We are all energy; we are a soul in a human body.

When we are born, we are just pure beings of love and light, yet as we grow, we become separate from our completeness, our *knowing*, our intuition, because we live and learn by what we see, looking to others to give us what we need.

We become human and we become physical, living by what we are surrounded by in our physical world.

We all live by our name, our gender, our position in our family, in society, our jobs, where we live.

This is what we learn, that we are someone. In our being human, we often forget our spiritual self, our soul, becoming separate from our inner being.

We have all chosen to be here at this time, to help bring all of humanity to a feeling of love and peace, to flow freely down river of life, without struggle and misfortune. It all starts with self. This is our divine right.

Everything around us is just an illusion.

The messages we receive from society, and even from our parents, can create fear in who we are.

In our judgement, our fear tricks us into believing we are not enough.

There is no fear, there can only be love.

Once we recognise and know this, we can step out of the game, we can then feel our power and a sense of our own security in who we are.

Now the healing can begin.

We all have a right side and a left side. Our right side is our male, physical energy and our left side is our female, emotional, spiritual energy. Everything is relative and significant.

If we are living in separation of our completeness, our bodies will bring aspects of our suppressed emotions into our awareness.

By living in our *allowing*, our listening and trusting, will assist us to shift the stagnant energy from our energy field.

We are the universe, the universe is within us, yet we deem ourselves separate, believing the universe is unreachable.

We are everything and nothing all at once.

We are all just energy, living in a physical world. Along the way we get caught up in the energy around us, losing sight of our inner *knowing*, our intuition and our remembering of what we are.

We are born in our completeness, we die in our completeness, we just have to attend to all the challenges and the chaos, we deal with in our everyday lives.

> *We are afraid of losing what we have, whether it's our life or our possessions and property. But this fear evaporates when we understand that our life stories and the history of the world were written by the same hand.* —Paulo Coehlo, *The Alchemist*

If we can all just understand that we have a power, a strength, a connection within us.

If we can take a step back from the chaos, and allow our souls to breathe.

We can then trust in our listening and remember we are our perfection of love in human form.

We are a soul in a human body. Within our soul all we are and all we can be is pure love & light.

We each just have to remember to, **Let Our Soul Breathe**, and be guided on our journey, the journey that has been written.

We have to know it is ok to walk our path, our way.

Once we take that first step, the universe responds everytime.

Who are we?

We Are All People

We are all born of another human.

We are all the same.

Yet, we like to think we are not.

We all eat, sleep, drink and go to the toilet. None of us can survive without this.

Look around; we may come from a different country, have different coloured skin, speak a different language, but the fundamentals are still the same.

We all have yearnings. We all give ourselves a hard time. Telling ourselves, we are too fat, too thin, too fast, too slow, too …, too ….

We are judging ourselves by what we see around us, and often spend our lives in competition with others.

Although, we are all fundamentally the same, we have our own journeys to live. No journey is the same for any two people.

The purpose of our individual journeys is to bring us to a place of peace and love of our selves—unconditionally. For us to embrace, respect, love and honour who we are at every moment.

You may be married, or in a relationship but the relationship you have with your *self* is the most important.

As humans, we are naturally compassionate and caring towards others. But we also have to be compassionate and caring towards ourselves.

This does not mean we are being selfish, but that we are just giving ourselves the consideration of our value and acknowledgement of being here.

We have to have the strength and courage to follow our hearts and trust, and not feed the fear of guilt and remorse for letting someone down.

Life as a human is, and can be complicated.

We are all just energy, and energy should flow easily and freely. Our lives are often so defined by what happens in the physical reality, that we fail to acknowledge our emotional being—our souls. Our souls know. Our souls are our guide.

Before we are born, we decide when we will be born, who we will be born to, and what path we will take. When we are born, the *veil* is down, so we do not remember that we have all been here before, and have many layers of experience and emotion wrapped around our soul. We live in our fear and are not aware of our own power.

We all choose to come back to earth, to transform the negative beliefs of our abandonment, abuse, denial and betrayal of ourselves, to one of love. Our soul brings situations into our lives, to help us feel; bringing us an awareness of our negative emotions. As we feel, we acknowledge we can then have the opportunity to transform our fears into love. We just have to be in our *awareness* and recognise the messages that are being shown.

Within our physical body, we all have a centre, a left side and a right side. Our centre is our trunk which holds us together.

Our right side is our male, physical side. Our left side is our feminine, spiritual side. Surrounding our body is the non-physical, emotional aspect of our being, our aura.

The body is energetically divided into two parts—the right, male dominant side and the left, female dominant side. This is not a new concept, it originated in eastern philosophies like Buddhism and Yoga, and you can even find evidence in their writings that the Mayan civilisation was aware of the power of maintaining balance between these two opposite energies.

Each human being has both a right and a left hemisphere in the brain; the right side being female, the left being male. The left brain—or male side, controls the right side of the body. The right brain—or female side, controls the left side of the body.

Everything must be in balance, physically and emotionally, so that we can stand straight and strong from the roots of our being. From our foundation of self-love, we can grow and develop our self-worth, self-value, self-acceptance which leads to self-belief, self-trust, self-faith.

Imagine yourself like a tree. You have your roots and your foundation from which you grow your strength, your core. Your foundation must stand strong, otherwise it will crumble and fall. When you are aware you are in your divine power, you can branch out, reach out and receive all that you need to nurture and support you from a place of love. The emotional support that lifts and creates you; your *leaves* and *blossoms,* will attract all that you need. We are all souls within our bodily temple.

Within our core, we have seven spinning, bright, colourful chakras positioned throughout our body from the base of our spine to our crown of our head. These energy centres help to regulate all our bodily processes; from organ function, to our immune system and our emotions.

Each chakra has its own vibrational frequency, a specific chakra colour, each governing a specific function. The chakras reflect outward from within, surrounding our physical body with our emotional purity, our aura, our colourful rainbow.

When we are born, we are just perfect emotional beings of purity and love. Our soul is our perfect self, but as we grow, we lose sight of that sense of a perfect *self*, in our everyday lives. Our chakras become dull and sluggish, causing a deficit—holes in our emotional aspect—that can manifest as sickness and disease, or as self-doubt, and the stagnation of our being.

We are here to connect and reignite our self from within. To spin our energy centres freely; to be our colour and our light to ourselves, radiating out to everyone and everything around us.

Are you standing strong in your foundation of love?

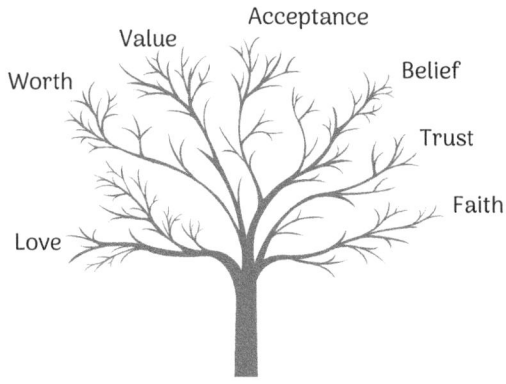

Living in total awareness of your worth

Or crumbling in your abandonment of you?

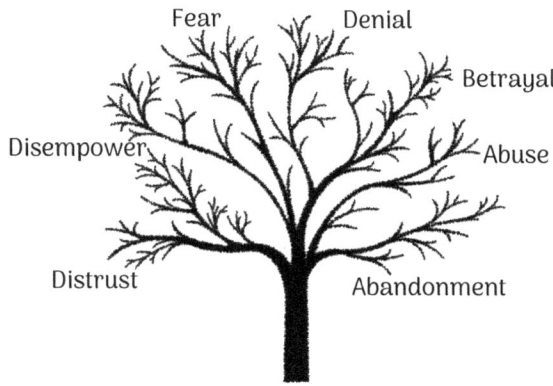

Living in denial of your truth and in control of your fear.

Our Journey

Everyone is unique with a unique journey. We are all here in the circle of life, to rediscover our inner being. We just have to listen. There is no right or wrong and there is no good or bad. It just is. All we can do is trust in ourselves, feel our worth, listen to our intuition, and let our souls be our guide. Remember to breathe.

In the womb, we are surrounded, protected and safe. We are complete. We are perfect beings of pure love, untouched, just being. We are cocooned. From the moment we are born, we become exposed, we become vulnerable, and just want to be nurtured and loved.

As babies, we are unconditional love and instinctively know that is what we are. Over time, we become separate and conditional in our being.

From a very young age, we learn how to seek love and approval, reaching out to receive from others. If we don't recognise this as children, and grow as adults, these behaviours can become self-defeating, and in time we lose sight of our significance. We strive to do better, to achieve, and to gain, often living by the expectations of others, and of our self.

We learn how to live in the physical, constructed world, and how to survive. Meanwhile denying ourselves of our emotional, non-physical aspect. Our just being.

If we continue to lose sight of ourselves, and our significance in who we are, looking to others for acceptance, and a sense of purpose. Our foundation can become one of struggle and conflict, rather than one of love.

We are constantly bombarded with what to do, what not to do, what to eat, what not to eat, how to do this, how to do that, what to believe, what not to believe. In between all that, we are surrounded by social media, statistics, fear mongering, how to upskill, better ourselves and make more money.

We are all caught up in a system of control. We have to work to earn our right to live. We are not encouraged to think for ourselves, and society dictates to us what we must do to get through one day to the next.

We are surrounded by solutions to every situation. Although there are many things in place to support us, and everything has its place and everything has a relevance. This can also be detrimental to our own ability to trust in our supportive mechanisms and our own intuition. Often taking away our opportunity to think for ourselves.

If we get sick, we go to the doctor; the doctor will order medication or tests for the physical symptom/s. Attending to the physical symptom, may just be the band aid, that does not attend holistically to the actual situation. Although it may help at the time, the emotional aspect is not attended to, the root of the problem. The tablet may take the pain, or the symptom away, the emotional aspect has to be attended to for the healing to take place. Otherwise, the physical symptoms may present themselves in different ways, until we get the message our body is trying to tell us. There may be many things in society to help and support us on a physical level, but that should not relieve us of our own responsibility to our emotional self.

We have a soul and an ego. The ego is our body/mind self, our false self, how we identify ourselves. The soul is our existential self, our true self, our feeling, intuitive self. Our soul is our perfection, our love, our inner being. Our ego is our fear, it is what we know, keeping us believing we have to prove our worth. It is easier to live in our ego, as that is what we are used to, keeping us in the game of life, that has served us over many lifetimes.

Our greatest fear is ourselves.

As children, we just play and dream, living in our imaginary world. As we grow up, our imagination fades.

We naturally have to become more conscious, more responsible thus losing sight or our significance of our being, having to focus more on doing.

We may have younger siblings, and may have felt in our innocence, we are not important or enough, as we have a brother or a sister. When we go to school, we learn about competition, fear, justification, and develop feelings of not being enough. We begin to look outside ourselves for approval and acceptance from others, rather than nurturing our own acceptance of ourselves.

As we grow up, we are surrounded by the expectations of others, especially those of our parents, in relation to careers, marriage, and the carrying on of family traditions. This constant striving can be painful and self-defeating. Our internal chatter can change with one thought of fun and laughter, to one of judgement and fear.

The silent voice, the chatter inside our heads goes un-noticed, as it is what we have become accustomed to. The chatter of 'not being enough, not doing enough, having to prove and justify' becomes like a stuck record going round and round in our heads. This can often lead to the mechanisms, that we often develop to try and help us cope in this world.

The addictions, eating disorders, ineffective relationship patterns, over-working, etc.

No one can escape the denial of self. It doesn't matter how much money we have, or how successful we are. Nothing is guaranteed outside of our self. Nothing can give us what we can't give to ourselves. We all have to be conscious of our inner chatter, and remember to know we are enough in who we are. We must all feel the way to our hearts, to provide ourselves with the feeling of peace.

We have all come here at this time, to bring heaven to earth, to know our perfection and how to be our love in human form. To raise the vibration of love of mother earth. One at a time. It all starts with our ourselves.

We are all energy in a physical form. We can touch, we can see, we can do. We also have a non-physical aspect to ourselves, our emotional and spiritual body. Within our non-physical, we are carrying the negative beliefs of abuse, abandonment, denial, betrayal of our inner being, we have been carrying over many lifetimes.

Our external reality, mirrors our internal world. We attract from our belief system. If we are not aware of our internal dialogue, we will continue to attract the same things and situations into our lives. These things become familiar, become our comfort zone, what we expect. Thus, why it becomes our norm. We become complacent, hence justifying our situation and limitations. Living in awareness of our inner self, is beneficial to how we live our lives, and what we are surrounded by.

Take action

Put your ego in the back seat, and ask from your heart. Trust. Listen to what you desire for you. Take time, sit in the quiet with yourself. Write down what you want, be specific. Make a dream board, a bucket list. If you want a partner, make room in your house. Make space in your bathroom, your wardrobe. Hang two towels in the bathroom. Make a cup of tea for him or her before you go to bed. Make a list of what you are looking for. Draw a picture of him or her looking at you. Visualise him or her holding your hand.

If you want to go on a trip. Write down where you want to go. How it will feel, the places you want to see. How you want to get there.

We just have to believe it is going to happen, whatever it is.

At every moment of everyday, we must be in awareness, listen, have patience, and trust in the process of life.

Change

All of us have been raised in a certain way, often having expectations put upon us subconsciously and/or consciously by our parents and our peers. We generally grow up doing our best to do what is expected of us, following what we are being taught, and so the cycle continues.

It is very subtle, as we learn as a young child to live seeking approval and acceptance from our parents. Often, we live our lives without recognising the patterns of behaviour.

As a young child, we learn to give our love and hugs to everyone around us, growing up giving to others and not to our self.

There is nothing wrong with this concept. It is just that once we are on the roundabout of life, it is very difficult to get off.

There are many books written about spiritual awakening and new age. A lot of people have different concepts and ideas as to our purpose and our soul's journey.

Our purpose, is to know how to live our truth and our listening of our inner *knowing*.

We, as humans are creatures of habit and we like to know the parameters to live our lives, allowing us to cope in what we think we know.

In reality, there are no boundaries. We just make them up to give us control, but then again, there is no control.

We all have to be open to the possibility of change at every moment.

We are all on our own journey of self which means something different for everyone.

There can be no judgement of ourselves or anyone. There can only be respect for ourselves and others.

All we can do is trust and be kind and compassionate, with love and understanding towards ourselves and others.

I am very philosophical and deep in my thinking.

All my life I failed to understand, why others could not see or comprehend what I could see. Growing up, living my life in my *knowing* and my connection to the universe, I felt a sense of completeness and isolation, as I was often dismissed as being strange.

As a child, I was told I could end up being alone, and to get my head out the clouds and my feet on the ground. I was made to fear me, as I was thought to be different.

Thus, when I felt my head was the size of the room and my mouth was small like a bird, the reflection, although I felt connected, I was scared to speak out about my *knowing*.

Although I had my inner *knowing*, I struggled in myself and my fear of being alone, by trying to belong. Living in constant conflict with myself.

All my life, I have lived well and I have lived happily. I have been very fortunate and have a very blessed life. Along the way, like many of us, I have met challenges, but am very grateful for who I am. To the world around me, I think I appear as the Karen they know, happy, friendly, compassionate and caring.

I may be all these things, but within me, I have struggled with me in this life, often wondering, what is it really all about?

I look around me. I look at me.

I journal daily. As I journal, I get confirmation and/or realisation of what I need to be aware of.

My book is about my writings of my self and my intuition; my inner *knowing*.

It is about assisting and supporting those who would like to grow in who they are, and knowing they are not alone.

It is up to each individual, and there is no right or wrong.

I have so much to say, so much inner *knowing*, in so many different ways. As I have written before, I live my life in my listening. Sometimes I get lost along the way, allowing my humanism to get in the way.

I will try and share with you what I know in a way you can understand and get it, giving you examples of what I experience every day.

Often when I have had a significant shift in my energy, I will find small amounts of money; 5 cents, 10 cents, 20 cents, occasionally I will find $1, $2 coins. All small change. Money lying on the ground. This is the universal energy letting me know there has been a shift in my energy field. The shift signifying *change* in my life.

There are messages all around us, that we may, or may be aware of.

I manage a motel. Recently I was upstairs in my apartment when, unbidden, I went downstairs to the office at random times. Each time I did, a car drove in, to check in. This is synchronicity.

Recently, I was thinking about making a pizza in my air fryer, I opened up Facebook and there was a post about making pizza in an air fryer.

I can be asking myself something or wanting confirmation about a situation, and as I am thinking my thoughts, a bird will call, a gecko will chirp, a dog will bark, or a siren or horn will sound. This happens regularly.

This is our soul, the universe getting our attention.

How often do you think of someone, and they call or message you?

We just have to be in our awareness of our listening.

Sometimes, when I get messages, the confirmation is very subtle, but it is there.

I am not a spiritual guru. I am just me, living my journey.

One thing I do know, is that when we question something. That something is our self.

When I questioned, should I or should I not write this book, I was exposed to many posts in regard to how to be an author.

I take this as confirmation, the universe saying Yes!

So here we go.

Not long ago I was listening to music when two songs played one after the other: Two Out of Three Ain't Bad by Meat Loaf – 'I Want You, I Need You, But There Ain't No Way I'm Ever Gonna Love You'. We all believe if we love ourselves, we are selfish, yet we cannot live in this world without ourselves.

And then: Almost Here by Delta Goodrem & Brian McFadden – 'You're Only Almost Here'. We are almost where we want to be, but we put other commitments or barriers or our resistance to ourselves in the way.

Both songs very significant in relation to how we all perceive ourselves in this world.

We are not, and never will be alone. We just have to know this, and allow ourselves to let go of what we perceive is our reality and open ourselves up to what is.

Recently I finished reading, *The Alchemist* by Paulo Coehlo for the second time.

We all have to allow ourselves; to know we are our own personal legend and we are our own alchemist, following our journey. To find our own way to our treasure, to know and understand our love of our self and our connection to all things in the universe.

As I sat down to start writing, the song playing was, The Alchemist.

There are messages all around us at every moment. We just have to listen.

Open the door to being aware of what is being shown to you.

I will take you on my journey of awareness, that I encounter at every moment.

Some may think, it is just coincidence, but it is about synchronicity and being conscious.

Today was my day off. My day started with an appointment to get my eyebrows tinted. I had a conversation with the girl who did my eyebrows about being awake and being conscious. I then went for a coffee and a man and a boy parked not far from where I was sitting. I then went for a 10km walk up to the lookout. On my way back, a few hours later, outside a house, I saw the same man and the boy I had seen four hours earlier on the main street. I then went to the supermarket.When i went to pay at the self-serve checkouts, of which there were many free, the one I chose was a cash/card check out and there in the cash dispenser, was lying 20 cents. Later on in the afternoon, I walked into town and as I walked along, I found 5 cents on the ground. Then I passed a girl, I had seen earlier that day.

All that I have written, is random acts of the day, it is also my soul showing me the synchronicities of life and my listening to my guidance and following through.

I am currently travelling Australia, just me and my van, Turtles. During my first night in my van, I padlocked my bicycle to a tree. Overnight someone drove into the park, cut the padlock and stole my bike. Apart from it being a real inconvenience, the message for me was to know how to feel safe and secure in myself. I am just about to embark on a solo journey travelling Australia, that brings up feelings of apprehension and vulnerability. It is about me being vigilant in knowing I am protected and looked after wherever I go and whatever I do and that it is ok to take responsibility of me.

As a child, I was made to believe I could not rely on myself to feel safe and secure. I had to deny myself of my inner *knowing* to belong.

I was also delayed leaving the town I was in, by a couple of days. Perhaps I was being stopped for a reason. If I had left the town on the day I was planning, something may have happened to me on the road.

There is always a message in everything. We just have to be in awareness and trust in our ability to listen to our self, rather than getting frustrated or upset.

When I realised the significance of what happened, I went for a walk and guess what I found, change? A five cent coin and a ten cent coin. As always, confirmation.

When we are on track, we align with the universe and it sends us signs for us to notice.

Nothing is a coincidence and everything happens for a reason.

Like, as I was writing this, the bird was chirping outside.

We all just have to trust and listen.

I am truly grateful and humble in my *knowing*. Growing up, I thought everyone was the same as me, with the same understanding. Our *knowing* is within all of us.

When we open up to ourselves, we go through a realisation of;

> *'I am doing this, I am living my life for me. I honour me, I value me.' It is a wake up to our being and our soul rejoices.*

This journey of self, is one of strength, courage and listening to our inner *knowing* and trusting.

Life is amazing at every turn. Our energy and our vibration are our reflection. As we live in our awareness, we shine, we live.

By taking stock of our allowing and responsibility of ourselves, and being in our allowing, brings on a new phenomenon for each of us. We just have to in the acknowledgement and acceptance of this.

Although, we cannot change the past, we no longer need it to serve us. We no longer need to allow our past to dictate our future.

We can allow the change and allow our feelings to keep pace with ourselves in where we are. Letting go, our need to live by the expectations of others. We become fully embraced in our authentic self.

By doing what we think is right for ourselves and by following our heart. We have the strength to wield our sword, slashing through the forest to get to our oasis. That is our direction.

After spending our lives in confusion and separation, we can now recognise our ability to be with ourselves and feel at peace with who we are.

Never underestimate or dismiss your significance, and the difference you are making just by being who you are, and shining your light.

Breathe

We fill our days with work, play, eating, drinking; belonging to something or someone. In between these times, we find ways to fill the voids with other activities, rather than sit in our own quiet, and with ourselves. Often looking to others to give us the credibility, we do not give to our self.

We are so busy running around getting somewhere, we often do not give ourselves the opportunity to know how to listen to the messages around us.

We may think we are lazy not doing something. The truth is, we are here to be the best we can be to ourselves. Sometimes in that moment, all we have to do is just sit and breathe.

Often, we are so busy trying to appease others, serve others, fit in, do what is expected, we lose sight of our own significance.

As humans, we like to control, or think we can control our emotional self, by suppressing and burying our negative thoughts of ourselves, finding ways to avoid feeling.

Some of us live in the constant daily dramas, or by filling every moment of everyday to devoid ourselves having any time to feel.

We are like the chrysalis before the transformation of the butterfly.

No one can heal us, transform us, remove us from the situation we are in our life, until we are ready to take that step.

Otherwise, we will fail to get the message or reflection we need to help us grow and move on in who we are.

We all have a choice, but the choice is ours to take, when we feel we can.

We all have to do what is right for ourselves at every moment, and have the ability to take responsibility for what is being shown to us.

To live in our awareness of our inner being, our soul.

It is about allowing ourselves to know who we are, as our self.

Many of us are wives, husbands, mothers, fathers, grandparents, teachers, nurses, etc, and although we are living our lives giving to others, we often do not know who we are to ourselves.

We are here to know who we are to ourselves. We have to be patient and kind to ourselves, and know it is ok to stop and give ourselves to our self.

We have to be willing to take responsibility of who we are, in who we are.

As we give to our self, we receive of our self.

In this moment of realisation, we give the space to others to give to themselves.

In this vibration of acknowledgement of our self, there is a sense of peace and contentment.

In this, there is no more searching, no more seeking, no more proving.

We create a ripple from each one of us in that moment, that spreads out across the universe, transforming the vibration of the planet, to one of love and truth.

There are messages at every turn.

At the end of the day, the message is always the same, the destination we are all striving for, is to return to our acceptance of our own love of self, and how to remember our magnificence in who we are.

Our bodies are our greatest messengers. They are all that we have that belongs to us. They are our best friends. We just have to listen and ask what they are telling us and be willing to take responsibility of what is being shown of our emotional self.

Nothing else belongs to us. We might think it does, but it is only temporary.

At times, we look for our *fix*, by working hard, pushing ourselves, drinking coffee, having that drink, exercise, going to the gym.

We are our *fix* to ourselves.

Sometimes, we just have to take time out and stop, to replenish our energy. If we do not listen to our inner self, our bodies will make us stop in different ways.

Everyday we all make a difference, just by being here.

We all have a significance and our reason for being here.

We are our significance and we are our reason.

We all doubt this. Every one of us.

We are surrounded by messages that are set to confuse us, numb us, hypnotise us into fear of our health and our well-being. Instead of worshipping movie stars, musicians, our doctors, etc, we have to know it is ok to worship and love ourselves for being here and showing up in our lives.

We often take on the energies of our parents and/or peers in our life.

As I discussed in the prologue, we have a right side and a left side.

Our right side is our male, physical self.

This is often influenced by male counterparts that have been or are in our lives, fathers, grandfathers, male teachers. Their energies can reflect on our ability to move forward in our own self, if we allow them to. As, often we may think they have a power over our decisions we make in our lives, thus affecting our ability to follow our own journeys under our own terms.

We are physical beings and if we are not living our lives in our own energy, we create a stagnation of energy in our bodies, that can manifest as a physical ailment or disease.

Our bodies are our greatest messenger, and will bring aspects of ourselves to our attention, in a physical way.

Instead of running off to the doctor, or the 'specialist'', we have to stop and ask ourselves what our body is showing us. What is it that we have to address within ourselves. Be our own 'specialist'.

All the answers are within us, we just have to trust in our *knowing*.

Our left side is our female, spiritual, emotional self.

We are spiritual beings, with a soul, living in a human body. Our vehicle that carries us through our lives.

As, we are living our lives by what is expected of us, attending to what we have to do to get through our day; we are often not giving ourselves the time or the respect of nurturing ourselves on an emotional level. Often putting our needs on hold, to attend to others. Not giving ourselves the time to feel.

Again, if we do not nurture our emotional self, guess what, our bodies will create an ailment to make us stop. But, often instead of taking our time to ask ourselves why we are sick, we can get caught up in the story, and the attention we receive from others.

We look to others to be our advocates for our reason.

We have to be our own advocates, our reason, our appreciation for being here.

No one else can give this to us, only we can.

We just have to know and understand this.

We Choose our own Lessons

Before we are born, our soul chooses the time in which we will live, our specific date of birth, our parents, the people we will meet in our lifetime, and many other situations, to assist us on our journey. Our lives follow a certain path, depending on where we are born, our family upbringing and traditions. Yet many of us continue to seek approval and acceptance, especially from our parents; sometimes to the detriment of our own lives.

We inherit certain patterns of behaviour and ways of being, often taking on the fears of those who were our caregivers when we were very young.

Our dysfunctional, emotional patterns sometimes manifest as illness and disease in the body and the mind. As our lives progress, clamouring fears drown out our inner voice and *knowing*.

When we are born, the *veil* is down. There is a *curtain* to close our mind, our memories, so, we don't remember what we have come for, or that we have been here before in previous lifetimes. As, we would continuously live in overwhelm.

We have come here this lifetime, to heal ourselves. Many people tell themselves, and or believe, 'I am not good enough, I feel a failure, I disappoint everyone, I could do better, I should do more, I am not important, I am hopeless, I am incompetent.'

The only way people know to overcome these beliefs, is to seek approval from others, please others, work harder/longer, go without, drink alcohol, smoke, overeat, and thus, people get sick, stressed, obese and cranky.

We all have a fear of being judged, reprimanded, and persecuted. This is because we live in judgement of ourselves. In reflection, abusive and ineffective relationships, are mirroring our own abandonment and abuse of ourselves, through living in constant judgement of our self.

We are brought up to put others first, and give to others; or be deemed selfish. In effect, we are being selfish to ourselves.

In the denial of self, we cause blockages in our energy field, that manifest in our body and/or our physical reality. Sickness and disease are a message that is being brought to our attention. For us to address the build-up of the negative energy, belief of our self in our system; our suppressed emotions. There have been many references made by authors, such as Louise Hay, Annette Noontil, and others about the link between our emotional state and the presence of sickness and disease.

Arthritis, represents resentment. Liver problems, represent anger issues. Skin irritations, bites, psoriasis, eczema, reflect issues of abuse, physically and emotionally.

Cancer, is a buildup of toxic emotions. Chest infections, bronchitis, pneumonia, asthma, are all aspects of our grief, the suppression of our loss or ourselves, reflecting our inability to breathe for ourselves.

These are all issues we are all carrying in our tissues.

We have a choice, to transform or not. The saying, 'Love heals all', should not be said lightly. Love does heal all, our love of ourselves.

Most of us are so busy getting through our day, in a robotic fashion, we are not in recognition of the messages around us. The universe will make us stop and listen.

We will have a knock, a car crash or get sick, or lose our job. That is not just 'bad luck', it is the universe, our soul telling us to wake up. We may have one or two little knocks, and then suddenly something may come out from 'left field'. That is us being told to wake up, or else.

Sometimes, we have to lose our external reality to return to our inner self. As, while we are living in our perceived reality, it can be difficult to see clearly through the 'fog'. If we are living in a belief of being 'incompetent' or 'not enough', we find ways to over compensate, to avoid taking responsibility of our negative belief system. We find ways for our lives to 'fit', which can often be a reflection of our fears of not being enough. We may have been giving all our power away to others, unconsciously trying to prove our worth, and need to be stripped to the core of our being, to come back to all that we have. Our self.

If someone is annoying or irritating us, it may be that their behaviour represents an aspect of our self, that annoys or irritates us, but also, is serving us. It is comfortable. If we judge others, we are in effect, judging ourselves. Everything is a reflection for us to see, if we want to.

When we judge others; we do not define them.
We define our self. – Earl Nightingale

When something happens in our life, often we want to blame the other person, rather than take responsibility of our cause in the situation. That is us playing the victim. Being the victim is no fun.

It may absolve us of taking responsibility for our unhappiness, or grievance. It still holds us in a negative way of being. The mind is very powerful, and yet, it is very clever at tricking us into believing we are not worthwhile. It keeps us in the illusion, the game of life.

We all must learn to love ourselves effectively. If, we continue to run ourselves ragged, the cracks will appear.

Take a step back and look at the situation, take responsibility for your part in the life you have created.

Whatever is happening in our lives, it is there as a gift. We must be honest and let ourselves feel our hopelessness, helplessness, anger, frustration.

These feelings are coming from our within, to wake us up and recognize, our inner being.

Are you feeling tormented or challenged by someone or something? This is yours to own. The torment may be coming from a feeling of guilt, or is indicative of your inability to forgive yourself of something therefore keeping you stuck in what you know.

Remember we are energy. Energy should flow freely around us. When energy becomes stagnant, it manifests in our being in different ways. We may develop excess weight gain, or chronic disease.

We will continue to live our lives, in a physical existence of ourselves, and not in honour of our completeness of our emotional self. We can shift the negative emotions allowing ourselves the possibility of being worthy of feeling our own love.

Living our lives with constant expectations which cannot be met, by others, or by ourselves, and conditioning ourselves into believing, we are not worthy, is a painful and helpless way to be. Allowing it can also become exhausting.

Unless, we can accept ourselves unconditionally, we will not be able to accept or receive another fully. Nor embrace the abundance and joy of ourselves and the universe.

Are you content with you? Are you conscious of your judgement and internal dialogue of you? Be honest and allow yourself to feel. Sometimes, we have been so hurt or abused, or have so much grief in our lives, it can be difficult to allow ourselves to feel, and to allow someone in our lives or, have the courage to take the steps to move on.

We may put up a barrier, a shield to protect ourselves from being hurt, becoming isolated and withdrawn from inviting others into our lives.

In this realization, we can learn to trust and allow our souls to support us to change and learn a different way of being.

Nothing can fulfil us, until we can feel fulfilled in who we are. No-one can love us, until we love ourselves. Our external situation is not static. It is a reflection of our inner being. Often making it up as we go along, sub-consciously; we as humans use our outer world for our fulfillment.

When we are living in our completeness, our reality will change accordingly. Remember there is no control. We just have to know that we are all that we need. We own nothing. Nothing and nobody belong to us and we only belong to ourselves.

As I was walking today, the song, by Crowded House, was singing in my head;

Somewhere deep inside, something's got a hold on you, And, it's pushing me aside, see it stretch on forever, stripping back the coats of lies and deception, back to the nothingness.

A message to each of one of us, to come back to ourselves, and stop pushing ourselves aside.

Who Are You?

Why are you here?

What is your purpose in your in your life?

We are so much more than our name, our gender, our job, or our position in society. We are spiritual beings in a human body. There are many aspects to who we are. In our awareness of our connection to ourselves, we become aware of our connection to all things. We are all one and a part of one universe.

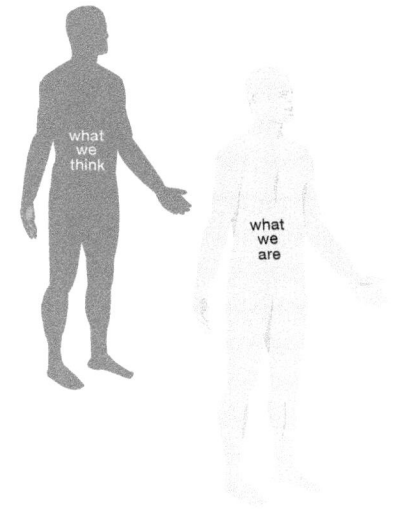

If you want to awaken, all of humanity,
Awaken all of yourself. – Lao Tzu

Our purpose is to bring heaven to earth. It all begins from our within. Our soul's will, is the little voice inside us. We just have to sit, give our soul time to speak, and listen. All our answers are within us. We must feel our denial of self, our negative emotions, and peel back the layers that have been wrapped around our soul, to know and remember that all we are and all we can be, is pure, unadulterated love.

As we raise our awareness, our energy, we can support others to do the same. To know of our connection to ourselves, we are then in awareness of our connection to all things, the animals, the birds, other souls, everything.

Have you ever met someone for the first time, but feel you know them? Our souls know, we just must trust and value our *knowing*. We could be talking to someone, or just sitting quietly and a gecko or a bird will chirp, a dog will bark, a plane will fly by, or a song will be playing, giving us confirmation of something. It is all about being in awareness of every moment and listening.

How often do we think of someone, we haven't seen for a while, and they call or bump into us? There are no mistakes, or coincidences.

Everything is meant to happen the way it does. Our souls know. We just have to know our souls are our guide, and will never do us wrong. As we recognize the small, subtle synchronicities, we open up to our awareness. Allowing our soul to show us of our connection to ourselves and others.

We often allow our fearful mind get in the way, and let it take command. As we have a need to control, and a need to make things happen how we want to happen. There is no control, there is nothing to fear.

Instead of trying to justify our lives, we should be deserving of our forgiveness of our not listening, or having an awareness of our inner being. Think about it, the birds, the trees, the animals all know their perfection, and are just being. That is a place, we can also be, if we so choose.

After many lifetimes of living in fear of who we are, it can be daunting to take that first step. Just remember we are well protected and the universe is waiting for us to ask for help and direction. Nothing comes into our awareness that we are not ready for, or cannot handle.

We must stand firm in our foundation of love and realise, that we no longer need the 'weeds', the fear that hold ourselves ransom. It is ok to stand in our power, and let our hearts be our guide. Find our way back to our being.

We all need the five basic human needs to survive; food, water, shelter, air, warmth. We all have to ensure that we can survive physically, and have access of means to meet these needs throughout our life.

We are all able to control, to some degree the outcome of this. We are not always able to control our emotions, or how we feel. That comes from within. The more we try and control, or deny how we really feel to ourselves, all we are doing is denying our purity and love.

There comes a time when we have to realise our need of self, of self-actualisation, self-reflection, self-fulfillment, personal growth and purpose. Life happens to us all, and sometimes we may have allowed life to get in the way, dampening our own self-progress. That is ok. It is about listening to how we are feeling and taking action in 'becoming' who we are.

We must allow ourselves to feel the loneliness that is crying out from our souls, our abandonment of ourselves. So that we can reconnect and align to all aspects of our being and have faith in our journeys.

For many, when anything comes up for our attention, the pain, the hurt, the anger. It is often deflected in some way, or medication is taken to cure the symptom. That is only a band aid. A short-term solution.

Trust in the process. Let go of the need to control or justify. We are meant to be where we are right now.

Sometimes events or situations can be delayed to protect us from harm. There may be synchronicities that have to fall into place. Things may not happen how we want them to, because there is something else meant for us. We may have to stay in a situation, that relationship, or a job, to get a particular message, or a recognition of what we have to see in ourselves, a gift from the situation.

We all have to learn patience and know.

'What is for us, will not go by us.'

We may not always be conscious of the good that is unfolding in our lives. It is all about being in communication with our self, at every moment of everyday, listening and learning to trust, rather than dismissing our inner voice, and asking others for their advice.

Be who you are and say what you feel, because those who mind, don't matter and those who matter, don't mind.–
Dr Seuss

As, we begin to lived a life of empowerment and awareness, others may retaliate and lash out. They are coming from a place of fear, and are threatened by our higher vibration of energy.

On some level, they know something is changing, and is different, but are unsure of what. Because they don't recognize the change, they go into fear. Just remember to breathe and stay in your power. Do not feed their fear. Step back, detach and observe.

Sometimes we may have to speak up to lift the vibration of the suppressed emotion to give us clarity to move forward or write down how we are feeling. We may have to look at a situation, and allow ourselves to feel how it is affecting us. Take responsibility to feel the 'anger.' By feeling our anger, allows the grief to come up. Underneath the grief, is our love, for us to feel.

By recognizing and understanding, that it is we, who create the blockages in our own lives, we can then take the steps to transform, align and balance our connection to ourselves. To live our lives authentically.

The greatest gift we can give to ourselves, is to be who we are. To allow our self to follow our truth and have trust and faith in who we are. Let go the negative emotions to feel our love and worthiness of our self to the core of our being. Listen and be conscious of what we are. Pure beings of love and light.

The greatest gift we can give to others, is to give them the space and allow them to follow their truth. We all come for this journey of self. How we come, how we live, how we go, is our choice. We can help, we can support, but we are not responsible for another's journey.

What we have to do is stand in partnership with ourselves, physically and emotionally, bringing ourselves to a state of peace.

All this time, our hearts have been closed. We can now trust our ability to open our hearts to our self.

When the heart is at peace, for and against are forgotten. – Chuang Tzu

We live in a physical/conscious reality, and everything in our lives is a reflection of our subconscious beliefs. We are energy and energy has to filled with something. Everything has a positive and a negative. Everything in our lives is meant to happen. There are no coincidences, no mistakes.

Before we are born, we choose our parents, and our siblings. They are a reflection of ourselves, and are our best teachers.

Are you in a relationship? Does it enhance your life or support you; Or is it debilitating you in some way? Do you feel connected, or lost? Are you content?

Be honest with yourself and ask yourself these questions. Allow yourself to feel you.

Some of us are men and some are women but we all have both masculine and feminine traits. Both have to be in balance for us to be healthy. An overly feminine woman, and an overly macho man are both lacking in balance. One cannot be without the other.

It is about living in honour and respect of the divine feminine. Our emotional aspect.

Feel your worth as a woman and know you have a voice. – Unknown

Women in particular, have lived in the thrall of male influences in our lives, perhaps over many lifetimes. We have also lived under a patriarchal ideology that defines what is expected of both man and woman.

It is time to balance our masculine and feminine energies, to be healthy, whole and complete.

Humans tend to be so busy physically that we neglect our emotional, spiritual energy. Often looking for a partner to give us what we are needing, or lacking, to support that aspect of ourselves.

To compliment ourselves will allow us to be complimented by another, changing the energy from a need or a lack, to an even balance of each vibration of each other.

Often, we are so busy feeding our lack, we will sometimes put ourselves in situations, that support our lack of self-worth.

Unless we are living in awareness of all aspects of our self emotionally and physically, or feel able to live in support of our self, we will attract someone into our lives who also needs our support. Reflecting our need to be needed by someone other than our self.

As we feel ready to connect to our own power, our soul will guide and support us to make the necessary changes in our life, step by step.

Fathers are usually the first male influence that we all encounter. Sometimes we may have fathers, who are not emotionally available to us. We may try to address our unmet childhood emotional needs, seeking our recognition and acceptance in our adult relationships.

It is as if, we have an invisible veil clouding our vision from seeing our love, or feeling of self-worth of ourselves. Especially as women in our equality to men. We do not need anyone's approval. We are all equal. It is time to feel the veil blow away, to recognize ourselves fully in our power as integrated, whole and enough.

Sometimes, males follow their father's emotional behavioural patterns and do not always know how to feel their emotions, denying their feminine aspect. Often, they will look for a female partner to give them what they are lacking within themselves.

History has shown that males have had to be more physical and a need to be in charge, or to take charge. Until they can allow themselves to feel, males will believe themselves to be superior to women feeding their ego. Their fears.

Thus, abusive relationships will continue. Women believing we need approval and acceptance from a man. Men believing they are superior to women.

We have to stand in our truth, honour and respect ourselves and feel our way to our heart. Physically, know we are strong and in our power. Emotionally, feel our foundation of self-love, feel worthy and know our value. Accept, believe, trust and have faith.

Why do we get sick?

We are all physical beings with a physical body. We are all energy. We are mostly aware of our physical being, but are not consciously aware of our invisible aspect of ourselves, our aura, our chakras, our energy centres. They should spin brightly, representing the seven colours of the rainbow.

Our aura is our magnetic field, that surrounds our physical body. If we are not living fully in our own self-love, we develop *holes*, negative emotions in our aura. The *holes* reflect negative energy, which can manifest in our energy field as sickness and disease, chaos and drama, in our every day lives. What we put out is what we attract, often subconsciously.

Living in the drama of life, keeps us from feeling or believing in our ability to return to our foundation of our power. We just keep going, struggling through the sludge until one day, something may make us stop, and make something change. It may be one word, one situation, an *aha* moment. Listen.

We have to let go of the fears, the negative emotions, that lie dormant in our body, impacting our everyday lives. We must allow ourselves to live fully in connection with our inner being and for our physical life to flow freely in every way.

It is easy to feel powerless around everyday ailments, sickness and disease. As a society, we expect to get sick.

There are doctors and hospitals all around. There are pharmacies on every corner. We are encouraged to be vaccinated. There are pills and potions for everything. We are all so caught up living a physical life, that we often neglect our emotional needs.

Everything has a message. From stubbing our toe to breaking an arm, or having a chronic disease. When we get hurt or sick, after we have attended to the physical situation, we must stop and ask our soul what the relevance is in regard to our emotional body. What do we have to acknowledge within ourselves?

It is the only way our body can communicate and bring aspects of our self to our attention.

If we all had insight and an awareness of our emotional needs to our self, there would be no need for the reflection of the negative beliefs from within, eliminating many sicknesses and disease. We can do much to heal ourselves and we can live in our power of our completeness.

Unless we are in complete awareness of ourselves emotionally, we cannot respect our emotional needs. The body is very clever and has a defence mechanism to give us a shake.

Often, when we get sick, or have a fall, it's the body's way of telling us to stop and take a rest. To listen and wake up to our inner *knowing*.

But often we are too busy and do not give ourselves the time we need to listen to the body's message. There is something that needs to be addressed in our emotional body to feel and attend to.

We have a right side, our male, physical body and a left side, our female, spiritual body. Our purpose is to live in complete balance of both aspects of our self, and to live in our love, honour and acceptance.

If we are out of balance, in any aspect of our self, this will reflect in our emotional body causing a physical ailment.

Any ailment that occurs on our *left side*—represents not living in respect of our feminine, emotional body or are not standing in our own feminine power. It may be an allowing of a female to dictate or influence us in our choices. Or it may be the carrying of a burden in relation to our mother, wife, sister, or a female aspect of our self.

Any ailment that occurs on our *right side*—represents not living in respect of our masculine, physical body or are not living our life for our self. It may be about the giving of our power to a significant male, often a father, in our life. Allowing them to influence us in our choices.

Bones are our structure that hold us together. We may develop fractures, bone cancer, osteoporosis, osteomyelitis, arthritis, if we are not standing in our power. Bone disease is a build up of resentment causing our structure to crumble and fall.

If we break our arm, this represents our inability to embrace or hug ourselves, or feel worthy to be embraced and held by another.

If we break our leg, this represents our inability to stand strong in our power, or may reflect the allowing of someone in our life, to knock us off balance.

Blood carries oxygen around our body and gives us warmth and love. Living in denial of our love, blocks our ability to live in our flow, causing blood disorders.

Teeth represent our emotions. If we are prone to toothache, gum disease, rotten teeth, bad breath, abscesses. We are in effect rotting in our emotional body. We are living in fear of acknowledging our emotions.

As, we are conceived by two people, one male, one female, and respecting our emotions. Their influence energetically has significance over our emotional body.

Our two front teeth reflect our relationship with our parents. Our front right tooth, our father and our left tooth, our mother.

If we have been abandoned by, or have emotional issues with our father or mother, one of, or both of our front teeth, will protrude and, or will be discoloured.

Toothache in our left side, represents our inability to respect our power emotionally and toothache in our right side, is showing, we may be giving away our power to a male in our life.

Problems with our skin, represents emotional abuse. If, we are susceptible to bites, eczema, psoriasis, rashes, hives, acne it may signify our disrespect of our feelings. A form of abuse, that is sitting, just 'under our skin,' causing the irritation.

Pain is a build-up of toxic emotions in our body crying for our attention to let go the guilt and betrayal of ourselves. To ask our self for forgiveness, to allow us to live in support and flow of who we are.

Nails are our protection. If we bite our nails, we are wearing away our protection. If we have continual nail problems, we have no emotional protection. We are emotionally powerless. False nails do not give us protection. We must have the ability to feel that we are a powerful being.

Hay fever and allergies, are irritations in our emotional body. The irritation is to irritate ourselves into taking action for ourselves.

Nausea and vomiting are a reflection of our inability to feel our worth. Our inability to digest our emotions. Vomiting is our body's way to trying to get rid of negative emotions. Diarrhoea is also the body's way of letting go of toxic emotion. Flatulence is our fear of living in respect or our worth.

Tonsilitis is a reflection of our inability to believe we can speak our truth freely, for fear of being reprimanded or dismissed.

High blood pressure, is about not being in our flow of our own love, and ignoring our own *knowing* and connection to ourselves and the universe. Putting our lives on hold for others for fear of being alone.

Headaches/migraines is the denying of having faith in ourselves to trust in our *knowing*.

Deafness/earache is not wanting to listen to our *knowing* and hear what our soul is trying to tell us. Again, living in the fear of being alone.

Constipation, is the holding on to the fear of not being enough. Not knowing how to let go, to feel our worthiness and be in our own flow.

Inflammation and infections are reflections of our anger coming to the surface for our acknowledgement. Under the anger, the resistance to our self, is the grief. Our loss of our own self. Under the grief, is our love. We must feel our grief, the hurt, to feel our self.

If we are carrying weight in our abdominal area, this signifies our inability to feel any of our emotions, and be able to digest our knowing of what we need.

Addictions are caused by the need to fill a void within ourselves with something else; food, alcohol, excessive exercise, etc. Reflecting, we are not able to feel a sense of fulfillment within our own self.

Tiredness is the body's way of telling us to stop and have a rest, at any time of the day. When we go through an energy shift, the body must have the opportunity to process and rebalance our energy.

Stop and breathe. Tiredness is also our resistance to believing in our ability to support and connect to our self emotionally.

We may be exerting energy towards another, to receive their approval. Giving away our power. Stop resisting our self. Sleeping will not resolve our tiredness, if our soul is tired.

Coughing is our body's natural reflex to dislodge something. Our feeling of inadequacy. If we have a continual cough, there is something that needs to be said or acknowledged by our self. Reflecting our own betrayal of our emotional body.

Mental health issues, anxiety and depression reflect our inability to trust in our soul. Trying to make sense, create logic, and control our emotions. Our emotional body flows freely. Let go and allow ourselves to feel from the core of our being. Only we can do this for ourselves. Only we know how we feel and help ourselves to bring our self back into balance.

Smoking is smelly and offensive. It is a curtain, a barrier that surrounds our self, to protect us from being hurt, or from allowing others to invade our space. In this avoidance, we are also avoiding the allowance of our self to receive fully in our own space.

Over indulgence of perfume is a sign that we may feel we are offensive in some way and are masking our offense at our self, with a toxic chemical, trying to cover up our own smell. Again, avoidance of our self.

Obesity is the denial of self. The abuse and abandonment of our emotional body. Trying to feed our emotions with food.

We also numb our emotional body with overeating, alcoholism, drugs, constant working, obsessive behaviours, excessive exercise, studying, and ineffective relationship patterns. Filling every moment of everyday. This behaviour is indicative of the running away from our emotions, and not wanting to feel.

The body cannot get rid of the negative emotion until we are ready to feel it. Once we allow our self to feel our worth, we can come to that place of unconditional love. There is then nothing to fear, and the body can release the negative emotions naturally and easily, and gently.

As, we acknowledge and release negative emotions, we may feel unwell, achy and tired. We may develop a cough or a cold-like symptoms, or a headache. There may be a heaviness felt in the abdominal area.

As we feel the emotion, we may release, we may cry, we may cough to the point of almost vomiting. We may feel anxious or nauseous. This is the body's way of telling us to stop and feel. We have to allow the emotion to come up. We must not suppress it. We are all energy; we are all in motion, and the body has a release mechanism.

As we have a shift in our energy, we may experience pain or discomfort in certain areas, as the energy is shifting, allowing us to move from a place of stagnation. There may be pain or discomfort in our knees or hips, as the energy has to become physical to allow us to be in awareness of the shift.

Most shifts are subtle, but have to be brought to our attention in some way.

As we release the negative, we make space for our purity and love.

Everything is relevant and everything is energy. Everything has a positive and a negative and everything has a for and against. We must live for ourselves, and against the negative beliefs and know we are the stars of our being.

People who have self-compassion and practice self-love, generally report feeling happier and more authentic in their relationships. Thus, they may feel safe and better able to assert their needs and opinions.

How psychological issues manifest in our life

Negative psychological and behavioural patterns, may manifest in our lives in indiffering ways, as we try to fix how we are feeling, by whatever external means are available to us. For example by going to the gym, drinking alcohol, or taking medication. What starts out as an effective coping mechanism may become ineffective and a problem in its own right.

Addiction could be defined as a chronic, compulsive behaviour, despite the negative consequences, that often can occur when we are avoiding facing, and feeling our emotional self.

> *... there is no coming to consciousness without pain.*
> *– Carl Jung, Contributions to Analytical Psychology.*

> *People will do anything, no matter how absurd, in order to avoid facing their own soul. One does not become enlightened by imagining figures of light, but by making the darkness conscious. – Carl Jung, Psychology and Alchemy.*

Often the concept of an addict or someone suffering with depression, has been associated with someone who is self-absorbed and self-centred. It has been thought that recovery must entail an ego deflation, a breaking of the self-focused pattern of thinking.

Whilst there is a sense in the latter statement, addicts only appear to be self-serving, while in fact their true selves and wishes are completely sublimated to their addiction, and/or their negative way of thinking until they can change the way they think and feel.

As well as this, people who are suffering can present as neglectful of their own well-being, and often have many behaviours which shows that they have an, 'external locus of control.' Behaviours such as people pleasing and co-dependency in its myriad forms.

Often people try to fix how they feel with drugs and alcohol, which can easily be classified as an addiction.

In addition, now many other behaviours are understood to be, 'process addictions', and we see people accessing treatment for sex/love addiction, gambling addiction, over and under eating, and the list goes on, ad infinitum.

Whilst the neurological reward system is activated more powerfully by certain substances, than by behaviours it is thought that the chemical process in the brain is similar.

Food addictions are normally classified as process addictions, even though substances are involved. This is due to the perception, that food is not directly mood altering or psychotropic.

It is not just the clinical world that has made the link between substance and behavioural addictions. People who identify as process addicts, (gambling, food, sex, etc), have adopted the self-help mechanisms like, Alcoholics Anonymous. The understanding of addictions, pioneered by those suffering with substance addictions.

If we don't like where we are. Change it. – Jim Rohn

In relation to our wellbeing and gender, the mind is in a near constant state of evaluation, judging and decision making on both a conscious and unconscious, or barely conscious level.

The thoughts that we often think, are the consequence of the dominant ideological order under which we live. By ideological order, I mean, our shared belief systems, values, and common culture. Those things, we learn through the institutions of family, school, religious society and the media as well as those things which are not just accepted culture, but are enforced by law.

Through these mediums, the dominant ideals of society go on to shape the consciousness of the people.

It has been often and well argued, that the civilisation of certain beliefs and opinions have served the dominant classes who control, both the means of material production, and the means of ideological production, within the psyche of the people, with the intention of maintaining the status quo.

An example of this social moulding is through gender. We witness the gendering of children from the moment they are born. Pink is for girls and blue is for boys.

Other distinctions and valuations of worth are made between race, sexuality, religion, body type and age.

In our patriarchal culture, many women have been conditioned to repress their needs, wants and opinions, and develop characteristics, such as vulnerability, while sublimating assertiveness and aggressiveness. Society views deviations from this way of being as being unwomanly and masculine.

This then leads to emotional dissonance and anxiety around the validity of our thoughts and feelings, leaving us with a sense that we have diminished value.

It is perhaps not surprising that women suffer higher rates of depression, anxiety disorders and comorbid conditions than men. This may be related to womens' cultural positioning, as of less value than men in the gender binary. This positioning as lived, means women are at greater risk of sexual, emotional and physical abuse. We are lower paid, do more unpaid work and have greater responsibilities as care givers. (World Health Organisation, 2000).

This is not to say, that men get off lightly with their gender role. It is well known that the rate at which men are killing themselves, is a tragedy of mass proportions. Their rate being at almost double than that of women.

The mass sacrifice of young men during times of war, for land and for money. Patriarchy is an issue which intersects with class and race in different ways.

Reflection

The Dalai Lama, when asked what surprised him most about humanity, answered:

Man.
Because he sacrifices his health in order to make money.
Then he sacrifices money to recuperate his health.
And then he is so anxious about the future that he does not enjoy the present; the result being that he does not live in the present or the future; he lives as if he is never going to die, then dies having never really lived.

Ask yourself;

Is my life supporting me?
Am I plagued with sickness or disease?
Am I aware of the messages around me?
Do I know how to be grateful to me, and see my value?

We are important. We are all significant and very much needed.

When we say thank you to someone for receiving something, we need to remember to say thank you to ourselves for allowing us to receive.

Everything in our life either supports us in who we are, or fills a void that we are lacking.

We may not know how to live in acknowledgement, or trust of our worth.

It is time to let go the fears and expectations of others and live our lives for ourselves.

As we shift and live in support of ourselves, our physical reality may change.

As we shift, we may not be able to stay in what we know, as it no longer serves us. We just have to trust, and ask our soul for guidance.

Look around, there will be aspects of our life that do support us, and there will be others that we subconsciously justify to keep us in what we know.

As we recognise our fears and let go and surrender to our heart. We will begin to feel a sense of peace and belonging from within.

We all think we have to be strong and show the world we are ok. The real strength comes from within and the allowing of ourselves to be present in our lives, at every moment of every day.

We must be conscious, as all we have is now. If we waste our time looking forward, or wishing things to be different, we will miss the message, the gift in every moment.

To be our love and our success, we must be vulnerable and allow ourselves to feel. To just trust and remember that our soul knows.

'Lead or follow, or get out of the way.'

Start following our own hearts, stop following another and see what happens.

When bees buzz by, the message is;

It's time to get organised and get to work on that idea. Approach our projects with commitment, diligence and dedication and we'll succeed beyond our wildest dreams.

As we participate in leading by our heart, we involve everyone around us.

Love is simple, allow it, feel it, receive it.
Stop holding ourselves ransom.
Let go and fly free.

Let Go

We have to take ourselves out of our routine and allow ourselves to reflect on our inner *knowing*, and remember. In our remembering, we can feel. To feel brings release, the tears. By allowing our self to let go and feel brings us back to love.

In our love, all we can receive is love. Nothing more, nothing less.

Are you ready to remember you?

It is time to reconnect to you and be in your completeness.

Imagine yourself, standing in the middle of the street naked, and feeling worthy.

When we are unconditional in our love to ourself, nothing can hurt us or harm us, as we are living in our acceptance of our inner wisdom.

There can be, no feelings of lack or less than. There is no need for gratification from another.

To think we have control, or want to have control over another in their choices or their lives, is living in our ego and is based on being conditional.

Instead of being deflective and living in judgement of another, or putting the blame on someone for the situation we are in. We need to step back, review the situation, ask what is being shown to us, and take responsibility of it.

Sometimes, we do not fully realise the impact of a situation in our lives at the time. We have to make time, to reflect and see past what is happening. There is always a message. To give us the opportunity to move past being the 'pawn' on the chess board.

Somewhere deep inside, we all have a fear of ourselves.

Our true happiness lies within us and our joy is ours to share with the world. Like the beckoning of the sea, our soul is beckoning to us to listen and remember.

We get hungry, we eat. We get thirsty, we drink. We get tired, we sleep. We are happy, we laugh. We are sad, we cry. We hug, we feel loved.

Everything is ever changing and we move through the motions of life every day. Yet any fulfillment we feel from an external source is short lived and temporary.

We are always with ourselves and are present at every moment. In this, there is no separation, we are of ourselves. We are of every moment.

In our hearts there is nothing. In our heads, we like to think and logicalise and put meaning into our day.

We have to feel past our logical brain and understand we are of this moment, we are of this universe.

We are in the ebb and flow of our lives. We just have to flow without judgement, without reason and feel our peace at every moment.

Be in our creation of ourselves and our own part of the universe and be in awareness and consciousness of our inner being.

Allow the universe to come to us, to guide us and support us.

Let go any resistance to ourselves, to get out of our heads, and follow our heart and open the door to our self.

To learn to let go the need to seek acceptance from another and live in acceptance of self.

In this we can come to our ability to accept and own the power within us.

Our body is made almost entirely of water, through which electrical discharges pass, communicating information. One such piece of information is called, love, and it can interfere with the entire organism. Love is always changing. – Paulo Coehlo

Our success is not based on what we have. It is based on who we are to ourselves. How honest and authentic we are being to ourselves.

The world as we are today, will still continue whether we are here or not. Our friends and family can still manage without us.

By learning to live in our acceptance of our own love, gives all the ability to realise their own acceptance.

Notice your small achievements in yourself, day by day. Observe your resilience, your stamina, and your empowerment.

We are all independent in our being, respect your independence within you.

The most important relationship we can have is our own relationship with our self, to be at peace in our relationship with ourselves.

Life Is Like a Jigsaw

We have to put our lives together, piece by piece, to see what fits, and how we fit into our lives. Only we know.

Everything has a vibration and everything has relevance and everything is energy.

I want to talk about numbers. The numbers 1 – 9. Every number can be broken down to add up to a single digit number.

Every number has a significance.
1. means new beginnings, new energy.
2. means relationships, partners, symmetry, equality.
3. means creation, creativity.
4. means our spiritual guides are around us.
5. means change, movement.
6. means on our way forward.
7. means standing in our power, powerful.
8. means abundance.
9. means completion, endings.

Every day/date, brings a new number signifying relevant energy to ourselves for that day.

For example, 25th November, 2024.

2+5+1+1+2+0+2+4=17 1+7 = **8**.

I just want to introduce, the idea of numbers, to bring this into your awareness. The little things, make a difference, and brings it all together, the connection of ourselves.

To bring you to an understanding of why I keep finding 5 cents, the money is, 'change'; The number 5 signifies change. Change in energy.

The title, *Let Your Soul Breathe*, $1 + 7 + 4 + 5 = 17 = 8$ = abundance, the abundance of you.

The number of pages is $182 = 1 + 8 + 2 = 11 = 2$ = relationships and symmetry, being in balance with you.

There is relevance in everything, we are our relevance.

Sometimes, it can be difficult to see what we need to be aware of; or be sure of the right direction, we need to take.

I have a set of guidance cards, which I use when I need confirmation or an answer to something.

If you do not have any cards, you can go to any bookstore or department store and buy some.

There are many different packs of cards available. When you go looking, see which ones you are drawn to, or jumps out at you.

When using the cards, take them out of the box and hold them close to your heart. Tap them three times, blow on them while asking a question to which you need an answer, or direction in something. Repeat the above three times, number '3' is the creation of something, shuffle and let the card fall out of the pack at random. Read the card. Feel the resonance of the message for you. Say thank you.

When our soul wants us to wake up to ourself, it will prod us to listen.

As, we are so good at being busy during our days, we may find we wake up at night, often at the same time, or possibly at different times. This happens, as our soul has our attention, we are not being busy, at avoiding ourselves.

I have tried to make, *Let Your Soul Breathe*, a simple introduction into you.

The question, you have to ask yourself; 'Is the pain greater, to stay, or to go.'

If you question life, and need direction or answers. If you have picked this book up, your soul is guiding you, to help you.

You may be surrounded by friends and family, but unless they have an awareness of their emotional energy, they may not be able to support you, in how you are feeling, or have any understanding in what you are saying.

It is not because they don't care. It is because they don't have the same insight.

Our journeys are very individual to each of us.

Remember there is no right or wrong.

We have to follow our hearts and live our journey for ourselves.

When something ends, it just means we have outgrown the situation energetically. Our outer reality, reflects our inner vibration.

When one door closes, another door opens. That is the natural progression of life.

When things are meant to happen, it becomes effortless and just flows.

We just have to be in our listening and our awareness.

When I have had an *aha* moment or a shift, often a police car will drive past.

This is my soul telling me I am safe and all is ok.

Listen to your thoughts or your judgement of someone or a situation, whatever you are saying to yourself, is your own thoughts of yourself. Everything is reflective and everything is brought into our awareness for us to take responsibility of ourselves.

Be extraordinary you!

Listen to, and feel you at every moment.

Our shift comes, in our realisation of our self.

Things to Ponder

When we cry, we are crying for ourselves. Our loss of ourselves.

When we miss something, or someone, we are missing the part of ourselves, that was.

When we receive ourselves, it allows us to receive and feel all of our self. And take responsibility of ourselves.

We are like a rotten tooth. We have to dig out the decay—our negative emotions—from the roots of our being, to fill ourselves up with our goodness and love.

In time, the clouds will begin to part and the sun will start to shine.

Sometimes all we have to do is digest ourselves.

We are our everything, know this, feel this, breathe this.

We have to cleanse what was, to allow what is.

We are all our channel for our divine power.

The old must be released, so that the new can enter.

Plunge boldly into the unknown of ourselves and be free wherever we are.

There is nothing in our day that has not come from imagination.

We are all treading water, existing in our lives.

Let go the need to be needed and live in our need for ourselves.

Nothing matters, we all just think it does, to give us reason.

We are our magnificence, we are our best, we are our perfection, just because.

We would rather avoid the pain of change, than to gain the pleasure of result.

Strive to do what is right not in the eyes of others but what is in our own heart.

Others thoughts are transitionary,

One moment they will love you, the next they will not.

Act what is right in our own heart, and there will be victory.

When we let go and allow ourselves to trust, we open the door to endless possibilities. The universe is waiting for us to take the leap of faith.

We have to let our soul speak, and let it be heard. We have to be raw and trust in our being.

We are so busy looking at what is going on around us, we are not listening to what is going on inside us.

Dare to entertain the possibility of loving all of our self.

Responsibility

I cannot emphasise enough.

Our soul wants us to grow and breathe for our self.

It doesn't matter how aware we are or are not. Or, if we are psychic or a healer or a spiritual guru, or just our self.

We cannot hide from the responsibility of ourselves.

I have recently been exposed to a situation, that really challenged me on every level.

I felt dismissed, abused and sick to the stomach. On some level, I dismiss and abuse myself. As many of us do.

Everything is a reflection. Everything is there for us to take responsibility of. To let go and grow.

We are all here to clear our own way along our path of life and no one can avoid this.

The situation occurred for me to realise something within me. As everything is there for us to realise something within us.

At first, all seemed fine, but then bit by bit, the cracks began to appear.

I began to feel sick.

The feeling sick was there for me to acknowledge that something was amiss and that I had to recognise the patterns of events of the now and the past.

We all have issues in our tissues, that have been there since our childhood and beyond.

As humans, we are naturally givers. Often givers to our own detriment, avoiding our own self.

The energy that was being presented to me, was like a leech. I was being sucked of my energy.

On some level I drain myself of my own energy.

I did not like how I was feeling. I was feeling isolated in myself and imprisoned. There is something within me that holds me ransom.

There were also people around me I was not enjoying being in my company.

These were both opportunities for me to recognise the aspects of myself I do not like that keep me feeling stuck. These people were also my gift for me to see myself clearly.

When there are strong energies around us, instead of dismissing or avoiding, we have to recognise how it is affecting us within, and take responsibility of our own self.

Once we recognise the messages and take responsibility of what is being shown. The person or persons, that have been upsetting us, will no longer affect how we feel, as the message has been acknowledged and healed. There will be no more energy causing angst or discomfort. The situation will disperse and there will be a positive shift in our energetic patterns.

Often, we may not see what we need to see, or recognise the energy that is being shown.

We may struggle in our daily lives, mentally, physically or psychologically. The struggle is what we become used to, feeding us on some level, giving us reason.

We go along innocently living our lives, until something is presented to us that we need to attend to on an emotional level.

Like a plant, that needs watering. The leaves lose their shine and curl to protect the plant from the sun.

Unless we water our self with our goodness, we lose our shine and our bounce and get sick.

We have to be vigilant and understand what is being shown to us at every moment.

For us to attract what we want in our lives, we have to first of all move through the yucky stuff, recognising there is always something in ourselves to be addressed, to clear the way for the new.

Be open to any opportunities being presented to us and be willing to receive.

As we shift, we may feel a discomfort somewhere to let us know the energy is moving.

We are our own responsibility and there can be no blame put on another.

They are there just to be our reflection, to bring things that are buried within us, to our attention.

Everything and everyone are a gift for us. Without them we wouldn't be able to shift. Be grateful.

There is an exercise you can do, to help address the people that are bringing up your discomfort, by talking to their souls and asking them what they are trying to show you.

- ~ Sit in a quiet, meditative space.
- ~ Close your eyes and breathe.
- ~ In your quiet space invite the people or person in.
- ~ Take your time.
- ~ Take the people who are reflecting your inner fears into your consciousness.
- ~ Take one in your right hand and one in your left hand.

- Then ask each one of them, individually, one at a time, what is their higher purpose.
- Wait for their answer.
- Then ask again to go higher, and again to go higher again.
- The whole time, be conscious of the messages for you and how you are feeling.
- The messages may come in words or a feeling or intuition.
- The messages will come.
- Take your time.
- When you feel, it is time to finish.
- Bring your hands together in prayer and hold the energy together at your heart space.
- Thank them for the reflection and the confirmation of what has been shown.

When you ask them, you are asking yourself for the reflection.

Overtime, you may feel uncomfortable, emotional, or unsure.

It is just the body's natural way of working through the shift in energy.

As you make time for your inner self and allow, you let go the resistance to you.

As humans when we experience a situation, we often get caught up in the drama of it.

Everything is brought to our awareness to allow us to take responsibility and grow in who we are.

I urge you to come to an awareness of what is being shown to you and let go the need to live as a victim.

Our soul is showing us at every turn, the way for us to return to our own purity and love.

I did this exercise.
- ~ I sat in a quiet, meditative space.
- ~ I sat with me, just breathing slowly.
- ~ In my quiet space, I invited these people in.
- ~ I took my time.
- ~ I took the people who were reflecting my inner fears into my consciousness.
- ~ I had one in my right hand and one in my left hand.
- ~ I then asked each one of them, individually, one at a time, what was their higher purpose.
- ~ I waited for their answer.
- ~ I then asked again to go higher, and again to go higher again.
- ~ The whole time, I was conscious of the messages for me and how I was feeling.
- ~ The messages I got from them after asking and listening, was to live in their own trust and faith of themselves.
- ~ The messages were loud and clear.
- ~ I sat with this for some time.
- ~ I brought my hands together in prayer and felt the union of the energy that was being shown.
- ~ I thanked them for the reflection and the confirmation.

That night, I lay in bed with my hands on my stomach, feeling the energy within me.

Throughout the night I could feel discomfort in my hips.

The energy in my hips is about the shift of energy and moving forward in my being.

I now understand the messages.

To stand strong in my own trust and faith in myself.

As I do this, I can then let go of my resistance to myself and allow.

As we let go our resistance to ourselves, we let go our resistance to others.

As we attract, we reflect; as we reflect, we attract our true reflection.

As our relationship with ourselves becomes healthier, this is what we will be surrounded by.

It is all about respecting our own relationship with ourselves.

It all starts from our within, to fully receive ourselves.

Cleansing

Every morning, I make up this drink. It sets me up for the day.

Morning cleansing recipe
- ~ 1 lemon squeezed
- ~ Stir in ¼ teaspoon of bicarbonate of soda
- ~ Add in 5 mls apple cider vinegar
- ~ Stir in 1 tsp honey
- ~ Fill up the cup with warm water

It helps cleanse your inside, like a pac man, it gobbles up the old cells, and puts the zing back into your step.

Try it.

Like anything, once we take that first step in anything we do, it opens up the flow, everything gets easier and falls into place, naturally.

Remember you are important. Do not allow yourself to be thieved of you.

Sometimes we just have to walk away.

Sometimes we just have to breathe and wait it out.

Sometimes we just have to get out of our own way.

Let the clouds clear for the sun to shine.

We don't fit into another's pocket. We fit into our own.

All is part of the process of our journey.

Feel your insecurities, they are there. Acknowledge them. Show yourself a little respect.

It is ok to be you. Trust every part of you.

We all have a fear of being a failure. It all stems from our childhood; from an innocent word or comment made from someone. From that comment we often take on the belief we are a failure to ourselves and others in some way. We develop ways of being to avoid being a failure through, 'good behaviour', or ways in which we get praise. As we grow, we do more of this as it relieves us of our 'fear of being a failure'. It becomes our norm, our drive.

And so, one day this way of being stops giving us what we think we want.

Like the calm after the storm. All our anguish dissipates. We take responsibility of realising we have been living with a fear of failure, deep within our being.

We can then realise we are a free spirit and our loyalty lies with our self.

We are ever on our journey of learning and decluttering our way back to our soul.

From my Blogs

Awakening

The other day someone asked the question, 'What is awakening?'

Awakening is the consciousness of our being.

Our realisation and awareness of our self, of our soul and our inner being.

The initiation of our opening up to our own self, Our awakening comes from our within, Not from outside of us.

Like a bud. It is the flower. Like a caterpillar. The butterfly.

Like the universe, we are the universe. We are all connected to all things.

Yet as we grow up, we become separate, from our inner being, Forgetting to belong to ourselves, Wanting to belong to someone, or something, trying to fit in.

Our awakening comes to us, in different ways, Our soul wants us to remember, our connection to our self.

We have to listen and notice.

The signs, the aha moments, That support us in our awakening.

Our journeys are not one thing. Our journeys are different for all, But we are all connected to all things.

We just have to trust and be willing, To allow in our own awakening.

As, we awaken and trust, We offer others the opportunity to open up the possibility of their awakening.

There is no right or wrong, no judgement, To awaken or not to awaken.

Awakening is different for all, It is not one thing.

It is not something we can see, Or explain.

It is a *knowing*, a feeling, our intuition.

It is about our own trust, to follow our inner guidance, And support ourselves in the steps we are taking.

We belong to ourselves.

All we have is ourselves, we are energy, we just have to be in the flow of our being, at every moment.

We Are Born

We are born as a baby, pure and wholesome, love and perfection, We are born with a body, within it, is our soul, our beingness.

As we grow, we are so focused, on where we are going, or what we are doing. We forget, that we were born, innocent.

What makes us decide, to take on responsibility, pressure to conform, live by expectations of others?

The person we are today, is the person we have always been. We may have weathered the storms, faced many challenges, worked hard, dealt with what has been given us.

Within us, is us, our love, our loyalty, our compassion, our own self. Do not put yourself down, or give yourself a hard time. Do not be disheartened, or feel less than. All we and all we can be is love, That is all we have to be to ourselves, at every moment. To remember our innocence, our purity, our love.

To Breathe

Without it we wouldn't exist.

When we are born, the first thing that happens to us, is our bottom is slapped, to make us breathe.

We may be male or female, who we are is our identity, it is not what we are. We are not our profession—that is what we do, It is not what we are

We get so caught up, in our daily lives, striving, achieving, stressing—what is it all for? All we have to do is breathe, everything else is irrelevant, in the scheme of our life.

Without breath, there is no one, yet for many, our bodies breathe for us We often do not even think about our breathing or the importance of it. We breathe in, we breathe out

In our respecting our breath, we are respecting ourselves, and our relevance.

We breathe. We are our breath. We are our love We breathe out our love, as we breathe. Like a pebble in a pond it ripples out and touches others. Never underestimate the power of our energy and our breath.

Open up to your beingness.

We are not, our doubts, our fears, our insignificance, our insecurities.

We are our own pure love of our self.

We all live by what we are shown, and what we see. Often it can be difficult, to see past what is in front of us and what we are surrounded by.

We are physical beings, with physical needs. We are spiritual beings, with a *knowing*, an awareness, a purity of self, yet we have become separate from our own love of self, often searching for the significance, from others.

I ask you to ask yourself, 'what am I here for'?

We are not here to suffer yet for many there is suffering on some level.

We have to look past this illusion and remember that Instead of searching outside of ourselves to receive what we need, we have to go inside and trust in our own guidance and purity.

We are here to remember our love and live in our vibration of love because that is what we are. We are all just love in human form. We are all amazing beings, we just have to allow ourselves to know the credibility of what we are and know to trust in our inner being.

What we are is inside us and no one or no thing can take this away unless we give our power to others.

Living in appreciation of who we are

We forget to do this. As children we are just *being*; having fun, laughing, playing make believe and enjoying life.

As we grow we believe we have to gain recognition and approval from others. I recently watched a wee boy just playing, splashing in the pool, having fun, just being himself.

That is a reflection of how we should be at every moment. We are not here to,b e the thinnest, the fittest, the tallest. We are here to live In gratitude, in appreciation and In respect, of our value, our worth, of who we are to ourselves. We are here to live in appreciation, of what we give just by being here in this world.

Give yourself a big hug and say thank you to you. Appreciate all that you are for being you.

We have been waiting for ourselves.

All our life, we are all we have been looking for.

To feel fulfilled in all that we are. To give us, ourselves, to live in respect, of our loyalty, to ourselves.

In this realisation, there is no separation, when there is no separation from ourselves there can only be connection to our soul, our being, our love

Everything around us has a message, to bring us back to ourselves. We just have to be in awareness of our listening. It can come in simple terms; in the words of a song, or a comment.

If we are in a relationship or have been in a relationship we have to look at that as if we are looking in the mirror for the reflection.

No one can commit to us, we have to make a commitment to ourselves to allow another to make a commitment.

It all begins with us; our awareness and responsibility to ourselves.

To Feel Safe

To feel safe and secure in all who we are, is the ultimate for all humans. I believe, before we are born, we have our own name that signifies who each one of us is; who we are.

When we are born, we are given a name, and over time we lose sight of the inner security, our soul's name brought to us.

We learn to fit into our name and become the expectation it brings.

I am on a journey. I am a nomad. I am travelling from eastern Australia to western Australia, solo.

Today, I was driving and memories of my childhood were very prominent. I was remembering eating certain foods; mince and tatties, roast pork. These foods, signify how I felt as a child — safe and secure.

I was very blessed and had loving grandparents and a loving family around me, I could feel the security I used to feel with my grandma, as a child. I felt very emotional and had a cry.

This journey driving solo is interesting and is challenging me to remember how safe and secure I am in myself. I am remembering how safe and secure I felt as a child, and who I naturally am. I am Pixie, that is my soul's name. I am living my life in trust and faith in myself. I am following me.

The name I was given at my birth, is me on a different

level. That is the person I was given responsibility for and expectation of. For many that is the person they know.

Although, that is the person that has dictated much of my life, the other side of me is the energy that has kept me going, trusting, allowing and believing — my inner self.

On this solo journey I now realise how much I feel safe and secure in myself. Until we can fully face ourselves, and recognise what we have lost we may not recognise our own ability to know how to totally feel safe and secure in who we are.

Do You Struggle?

Do you struggle with you? Do you feel you are where you are meant to be? Do you feel fulfilled in all who you are?

We all live our everyday lives in a certain way, often following what is expected of us, and what we think fits with everyone elses expectations. Not, giving ourselves our fit.

It is often easy to keep going with what we know rather than stop and take heed of how we feel and give ourselves our respect and appreciation.

Our lives are made up of doing, going, achieving. We are busy from the time we wake until we fall asleep. Surrounded by media and messages, we do not give ourselves time to feel.

Deep down within all of us is our *knowing*, our desires, our being. But we are so busy fitting in or living in fear of letting someone down we do not live in support of what we are.

Living our lives in justification and separation. Looking to others for acceptance. Our own acceptance, is ours to feel and receive. To live in trust and support of our own self.

This takes courage and awareness—to give our self to ourself. To remember how to fully embrace our love of our own self.

Be Grateful to You

Be grateful to you, for you; you are you and there is no one else, like you, feels like you, or is you.

We have to see ourselves in all that we are, see ourselves in our own uniqueness. Love, appreciate, and respect our ability to be everything to ourselves and more.

Take the pressure of ourselves to be what is expected and enjoy ourselves at every moment. Be grateful and fall in love with ourselves, for who we are. Live our lives in this *knowing*, in our *knowing* of our truth and our love.

To let go the control of believing we are not enough, remembering how to be our love to ourselves at every moment.

Every Door

Every door that we open to ourselves leads us to somewhere.

Whatever door we go through we go too. Wherever we go, whatever we do, all we can know is ourselves and allow our self to lead us through our own trust and love of ourselves.

Our journeys are our own to live. Along the way we may meet people who will come with us for a time but we have to allow ourselves to follow our own journeys.

Each one of us has a different route to follow. Our own love, our own understanding, our own respect is ours to have and live in.

We just have to allow ourselves to feel our own authentic love that lies within.

Our Worth

Our worth comes from us, we are our worth, our value, our love.

Nothing and no-one can give this to us. It doesn't come from anything or anyone, it comes from our being on this earth, or being our self.

We all have a body, we all have a soul. Our soul is our completeness, our bodies are our vehicle.

Whether we have $1,000,000 or $1 does not signify our worth, or our lack of worth.

Whether we are a top court judge or a homeless person does not signify our value. We are often taught to push ourselves to achieve, to compete, to be the best.

No one, is not the best, we are all our best at being who we are, yet for many of us this is not known, often living our lives in competition with ourselves.

We may have feelings of inadequacy or irrelevance because we are not top of the class, or have the slim body or whatever stories we tell ourselves.

The truth is, no one can be inadequate, because we are all our best versions of our soul at every moment.

Give yourself a hug and say I love you.

We Are Powerful

We are powerful beings of love and light.

Often we do not realise our power in who we are because we can be caught up trying to fit in, stay in a relationship, working to earn money.

We are often more used to giving away our power to others.

This post has been instigated, by a situation I observed. Today a couple check into my motel. They have been here before, she is older than him, she is a lovely, gentle soul. He is a man who likes to make comments, about being younger than her, quite derogatory comments at times.

This shows me that because she just accepts the situation she has no power in herself.

Whether she is so used to it that she doesn't notice, or she doesn't know she has power.

As humans, we don't always acknowledge what we put up with because it is either, not plain to see, or it is too hard to change.

What we have to understand, especially as women, is that we have power. We do not have to prove or justify this. We do not have to seek permission from a man to receive credibility, or worth.

We are powerful in our own right, so by walking away or seeing the situation for what it is we can then realise our power.

We are here to observe if we can live and understand that we don't have to give our power to anything, or anyone. Our *knowing* is enough. There is nothing to explain. It is just our own acknowledgement to ourselves of our power.

What Is Life All About

Living in trust of our soul leading the way and enjoying the ride.

Listening to ourselves, our intuition, and following through. Allowing, being conscious, recognising the process, being grateful to things just falling into place.

It all comes from our listening. Asking and waiting for all that we need to fall into place.

Naturally, it is about not abandoning ourselves staying true to ourselves, recognising our journey and our responsibility to ourselves.

We are not here to live in justification of or to gain acceptance and approval from another, or to seek appreciation or gratification. That is all part of an illusion.

We have to recognise our strength and commitment to ourselves. To dig deep and feel our own power within.

To breathe and live our life by allowing ourselves to live for ourselves, gives others the opportunity to live their lives for themselves.

Like a ripple, it all starts from within and spreads out to all around. We just have to allow and trust.

We Are Our Breath

We breathe, our body is the breather, we are the watcher. Sometimes we just have to surrender to ourselves and be the observer.

As people we just keep going, we just keep doing, because that is what we think we have to do.

Often we do not notice the stress, the tiredness, or we just become numb as it becomes the norm'

What we have to do is stop and surrender, and allow ourselves to receive support. We do not have to do everything. We are allowed to have help. It may come from a random person or when we least expect it, but when it does come allow yourself to receive it. Stop and allow yourself to feel the surrender of you.

When we show ourselves we can receive we can begin to receive in all areas f our lives. To receive your breath is to breathe. Is to receive you.

Who/What Are We?

What makes us who we are? Why do we function?

We all have a body to keep us warm, that just breathes for us. We have feet to stand. We have legs to walk. We have hands to touch. We have arms to hold. We have eyes to see. We have ears to hear. We have a mouth to speak. We have a nose to smell. We have a heart that beats. We have lungs to breathe. We have a brain to think. We have teeth to eat.

Do you ever wonder what makes us work? There is no switch to turn off and on. There is no power to plug into. We just are.

We are all of the same. We all have the same make up. We all have the same needs. We all dismiss ourselves.

Many of us are looking for that special someone, that partner, that something to belong to, that purpose.

We *are* our purpose. We belong to ourselves. Our soul is our lifeline. We are here to feel, to experience our love in human form in who we are.

Just stop for a second and be that special person to you. Give yourself a hug. Say thank you to you for turning up in your life every day, and for being you.

We Are Just Energy

We are just energy. In this realisation we can then begin to understand ourselves on a different level.

When we are born we are just pure love and light but as we grow we lose sight of our own significance, often taking on the beliefs and fears of others, without our knowing or being conscious of this.

If we can live in our understanding of our energy, we can let go the need to seek approval from another or the need to fit in or belong.

In our understanding of being just energy we can allow the shift of the dense stagnation energy we carry in our self. The more we can shift or let go of the illusion, the denseness, we can begin to live our lives in respect of our energetic being.

It is all about facing ourselves on every level and taking responsibility for our own energy. In this, we will become lighter, we can live in our truth, remembering our authentic self, allowing our energy to flow naturally. This is our natural way of being.

We are our magnificence at every moment, every turn. We just have to remember this.

It Is in Our Allowing

For each of us to allow ourselves to live our lives, to be in our lives, to be what we want to be, to go where we want to go. We may be doing this sometimes but in the doing we still have a resistance to our allowing.

Our power comes from our allowing of ourselves for ourselves in our human existence. We all have a need to be needed or to be better or to hide in our, own ability to be who we are.

We often hide in our vices whether it be work, drugs, alcohol, exercise, to avoid recognising our need to be needed. Although we may avoid a vice, like alcohol or drugs until we recognise our patterns of behaviour, it does not stop us from living with the need to be needed. It is better to accept our vices rather than avoid them as often, we replace one vice, with another, generally without recognising our justification.

In the acceptance we can allow ourselves to take responsibility of our allowing of our self. We all just have to know that just by being who we are we are enough.

There is nothing or that can give us this but ourselves. We are all just energy, we have to stop giving our power to food, alcohol, drugs, relationships, our image, our finances, our abilities and know our power lies within us.

It is about our acceptance of ourselves and acceptance of our power. Living in our own acceptance is only the power we need. We are our completeness in who we are, in our connection to ourselves.

We just have to remember.

One Day

One day we are a child, the next we are an adult, left wondering what happened.

Many of us arrive at adulthood not knowing how we got there or what is expected of us, or what we should be doing. Often living on automatic pilot trying to get through one day to the next, not knowing how to deal with what is being thrown at us every day.

Some of us have to juggle being a parent with work commitments. In between cooking, cleaning and breathing, being human is challenging. Wondering if we are doing it right but often just faking it, 'til we make it.

We are all in the same boat. No one definitely knows. Nobody is privy to having it right. We can all pretend we do. We can all have our own philosophies. We are all born the same. We all have a soul and a body. We have no right to judge another or make them wrong.

We have all come here to be human. That means something different to everyone else. What we can do is have compassion for ourselves in our compassion for ourselves.

We can have compassion for others. We all have challenges. We all have to respect ourselves and each other, and let go the judgement. All we are and all we can be is love. All we have to know is to be our love to our self and to others.

We Are Spiritual Beings

We are all spiritual beings. We all have a soul, our inner *knowing*, living in a physical body,

Everyone is spiritual, no one is not. Many do not know or realise this, living in a physical world, becoming separate from their own spirituality,

Our awakening is our realisation of our own spirituality. It is a process of our awareness. It is us opening up to what we are.

Each one of us is on our journey of self, we agreed to this before we were born, yet when we are born, we forget.

For many it maybe too difficult to take responsibility to allow the process, to remember all we are is a spiritual being.

Every day, we are bombarded with messages, some obvious, some cryptic; we are controlled, suppressed and denied of our ability to remember that all we have is ourselves.

Our bodies are our vehicle into this world our bodies bring messages to us in the forms of physical disease and ailments as this is all we can rely on.

There are no mistakes. Disease and ailments are a reflection of our stagnant, dense energy, yet we often do not associate the messages our body is trying to tell us.

We go to specialists, doctors, psychologists expecting them to give us the answers. All the answers lie within us. All of us have the ability to listen to what is being told to us, yet, many would rather live in, the drama, the chaos, the struggle rather than know to take responsibility, to remember our own spirituality.

As humans, it is sometimes easier, to allow ourselves to be submerged in the needs of others. All we are doing is denying ourselves the permission to be our own spirituality.

We all have come here, to be our natural love, in human form. For this to be, we have to understand, we are spiritual.

We are more than our physical appearance. We do not have to be in competition. We are all complete in who we are. No one is any different from another. It is time to remember.

We Have to Be Flexible

In our appreciation of ourselves we cannot appreciate ourselves because of one thing, or because of who we are. We have to appreciate ourselves, our journeys, or living our lives for being here.

This morning, I woke up with the message, 'Bloom'. Be my bloom, to bloom in who I am.

We all have to know it is ok to be our own bloom, to be our purpose, to shine in what we are. We are not one thing, we are everything.

We are not another's belief, we are our own belief. We are our everything to ourselves. We are our own significance, yet often we look for that from others, losing sight of our own being.

We are what we are. We are unique. There is no one else like us. We cannot compare. To compare is to become separate, to deny ourselves of our own uniqueness and qualities, and our appreciation of our self. Allow your self to appreciate you.

In Bloom

Yesterday I wrote about being our bloom. Today, I opened up Spotify and a suggestion popped up — Joy Oladokum, 'In Bloom'. There is a message in this; I am, we are, 'In Bloom.' Later I was making a fried egg for breakfast, in the white in the pan there was a heart, showing me confirmation.

As I was walking along the beach tonight thinking about the writing of this post, there was a crow standing right beside me. As I was writing my post in my head he made a loud 'caw' — confirmation. As I was writing this a gecko chirped — confirmation.

We have to be in our listening and awareness to the many messages there are around us. We are all energy. We are all connected. We just have to be open to the messages that are given to us every moment of every day. We all have to know we are stronger than we think. We all have to understand, that evrything is presented to us when we are able to receive it. We are only given what we can handle.

Never dismiss or deny you. You have the strength and the courage to attend to whatever is presented to you.

Remember, we are all here to live our journeys in our trust of ourselves.

This Is for Everyone

Live and know how to give your magnificence to you. Know it, feel it, be it at every moment. We are like a jigsaw, we are all a piece of the puzzle of life. We all have a purpose just by being here.

Whether we sing or dance, are the CEO of a company, have 10 children or spend all day in bed, we each form a minute part of this magnificence. That has a relevance beyond our understanding.

From the moment we are born we become separate from our *knowing*. We lose our sense of our purpose, often spending our lives in our own competition, searching for our significance.

We listen to the opinions of others. We justify our existence by what we see in our self and in others, living in our own judgement of self.

Every now and then we may catch a glimpse of what we remember, then our minds get in the way, bringing in doubt and fear, allowing the need to belong to take over.

We just have to know that we are our own magnificence, we are our own uniqueness and without us being here the puzzle would not be complete.

To feel, to know, to be our love

As children, we just know, everything will be ok. We have no agenda, no time restrictions or anywhere else to be. We just play, enjoy, imagine and believe that everything is possible.

As we grow, doubt creeps in, along with beliefs of 'I can't' or 'I am not enough.' We learn to compromise and be needed, putting conditions on who we are. Over time life becomes a routine and familiar. It becomes comfortable and we 'fit in' to what is going on around us.

When we try to take any responsibility for ourselves, it is often met with upset and disgruntled emotions. While we are 'fitting in', we are allowing ourselves to be needed.

As we shift our way of being, the other person or people, feel the void and don't like it, so they put blame on us for any upset they are experiencing.

As we grow, our ego feeds us with the need to be needed. Sometime during your life, you may have wanted to do something for yourself. To step into your own power, but have backed down, because you *like* being needed.

Sometimes, you may throw yourself into a relationship with another. This may be to avoid you feeling your own grief, or allowing you to acknowledge your own denial of self.

Are you ignoring you?

In this life, it may be easier to focus on what has to be done to get through the day, than to stop, listen and connect to yourself.

The separateness from self is what you have come to know and feeds the need to constantly be doing something, to give you a sense of satisfaction. It fulfils a need to be needed by others. An acceptance.

When that situation, person or event goes, we will often look for something else to fill that void, rather than feel the emptiness.

Nothing can give us what you are not giving ourself.

The only thing you have at every moment of everyday is you.

Love is all we are; and all we can be.

It sounds so simple. It is. Yet, we all hide from being our love. We make life complicated, conditioning ourselves to live in our daily lives. Losing our ability to trust in our journey. Pushing ourselves to prove our worth. Giving to others, before we give to ourselves.

We are all guilty of abandoning, denying, betraying our own *knowing* to receive approval from others.

All we are is just energy. Our natural way of being is to just flow with ease through our daily lives, without any bumps. Our beliefs of not being enough, is just a perception. In that perception we carry our abandonment, denial, betrayal, our negative self-talk. I should … the bumps.

What we carry in our emotional energy, we reflect in our everyday reality. In between the chaos or the judgment, there are glimpses of ease.

How would it be to live your life of ease, with only glimpses of chaos or anguish?

Be Your Best Friend

It is time to take a step back and give yourself permission to be you; to receive all of you.

We all want to be free, often looking outside ourselves for that freedom, whether it be financial or to fly free. The freedom comes from within. Once we let go of the ego mind, and live from our hearts and trust what we are. Our reality will shift, bringing us to a sense of peace. That is true freedom.

Many of us have been here many times before and will continue to come back, as we so choose. There is no death. Our souls never die. We just move from physical to non-physical energy.

We choose when we come, we choose when we go. Remember there are no mistakes.

We all have to let go of the responsibility of others, and take responsibility of ourselves. Understand that everyone's journey is unique and it is not our responsibility to get in the way.

We can open our minds to the infinite possibilities of what we are.

We must allow ourselves the opportunity to just be and trust.

Remember nothing can give us what we can't give ourselves, nothing can fulfil us, until we feel our fulfilment of our self. As everything else is temporary.

Presence is the key to evolution. We hold it in our hands.

It is time to reconnect to our soul and be grounded in mother earth. We are divine miracles of love and light. Believe it.

There should be no such thing as sickness or disease. They are caused by our fear and blockages in our conscious mind.

Our body is the barometer of our soul.

Every physical ailment, from stubbing our toe, to cancer is a reflection of our emotional body.

Everything around us is a mirror image of our beliefs and we attract everything into our aura to acknowledge and transform, to return to our love of self.

All we are and all we can be, is energy. Like attracts like. It is now time to clear away the cobwebs of that which no longer serves us.

People come into our lives, and leave again to show us what we are reflecting from within. They are one of our greatest gifts. Every moment is a gift.

Our lives are a journey of many things; ups and downs; sadness; happiness; celebrations; loneliness. Every moment is different from the last.

We have all chosen to come here and transform our negative emotions, of abuse, abandonment, denial, betrayal of our self.

We are here to experience what our life has to offer.

We must detach from the illusion, and find our freedom from within.

Life is a flow of changes, people come, people go.

The one thing that doesn't leave us, is ourselves.

Reach out and be your best friend. Be your power; your passion your essence of you. Feel you; do not fear you; love you.

I invite you to take this journey to you; let yourself feel.

This journey of self can be challenging and is a process.

You may be taking yourself to a place you have forgotten. The first step is all down to you;

'Within you, is a stillness and a sanctuary to which you can retreat at any time and be yourself.' – Herman Hesse

Are you ready to live your life in support of you; to feel your loss; your loneliness; to live in honour and respect of your love and worthiness and know;

'I am all that I am; I am perfect, whole and complete.'

Let's Go

Open The Door to You

'Whoever tries to help a butterfly come out of its cocoon, kills it.

Whoever attempts to help a bud emerge from the seed, destroys it.

Whoever tries to awaken consciousness in someone who is not ready, confuses him.

There certain things that cannot be helped, they must happen from the inside, out.' – Unknown

Healing Practices and Techniques

The meditations and practices outlined in this programme will take a multidimensional approach, encouraging spiritual development, as well as a change in thinking. A releasing of negative patterns, and a starting point on which to base a spiritual, mental, physical and emotional healing.

Breathwork

Imbalance in our nervous system is responsible for a great deal of *disease* and *dis-ease*. When we try to regulate how we feel using unhealthy or ineffective coping mechanisms, like unhealthy eating habits, addictions and co-dependant relationships; we create even more stress for ourselves.

Breathwork, along with chakra meditations and the saying of affirmations that I have outlined will:

~ Enable you to overcome barriers to meditation practice. You can practice these tools whenever and wherever you are; even with work and childcare commitments, you can fit this in with your routine, while walking, driving, washing the dishes.

~ Equip you with meditation tools that can enhance your well-being, fostering feelings of self-love and self-acceptance.

~ Empower you to make positive changes in your life.

Through a combination of conscious breath work, chakra meditation and visualisations, we will learn to calm our flight and fight processes; relieve ourselves of pain and reduce the level of cortisol in our system; nurturing a sense of peace and feelings of security.

It may seem too good to be true, or you may experience resistance to these ideas, because they just seem too simple. Don't be put off by how simple and easy it is. Breathing practice is one of the most time effective, and cost effective of all meditative techniques.

Breathe

Bringing our bodies back into balance, helps to regulate our physiology.

We all know how to turn up every day in our lives. We all know how to think. How we think, affects how we feel and how we feel, affects how we think. We are all energy in motion; our hearts beat; our body breathes; but we are not conscious of the psychology of our bodies. What is going on at every moment of every day; and are not often aware of how much we are not.

As we breathe through the centre of our chest, our heart becomes auto coherent, bringing synchronicity to our body. Helping to quieten the mind from where we can focus and fell. This brings us to a positive, emotional state of being. A place of contentment and a sense of peace.

Breathing Exercise

- ~ If, you can, sit and close your eyes.
- ~ Focus and breathe through the centre of your chest.
- ~ Rhythmically breathe large, smooth, even breaths.
- ~ Breathe in, counting to four.
- ~ Breathe out, counting to five
- ~ Repeat, each time adding an extra breath in, and an extra breath out,
- ~ Until you are breathing in to the count of six,
- ~ and breathing out to the count of 8
- ~ Stay at this count of six breaths in, eight breaths out,
- ~ Until you feel a sense of calm.
- ~ Open your eyes, and feel your peace within.

Mindfulness Practice

'Hold a thought for 17 seconds and the laws of attraction kick in. Hold a thought for 68 seconds and things move. Manifestation has begun.' – Abraham Hicks

Mindfulness Meditation works by short circuiting the preoccupation of the mind, the stream of consciousness is broken, and the accompanying feelings lessen.

When trying this practice for the first time, it can be quite unsettling to become aware of the huge number of thoughts coursing through the mind. Particularly the amount, that are negative judgements or fear based.

It is important to remember that thinking and evaluating is the function of the mind and that this is completely 'normal.' The mind is a tool and we can use it to create a world in which we can be joyful, appreciative and healthy.

Affirmation: *I know that my mind is a powerful healing tool.*

During mindfulness meditation, we focus the mind in a non-analytical way on the breath, a mantra or word, or some aspect of the environment; for example, a candle or soothing music.

When the mind wanders, as it will, we gently bring it back to focusing.

Mindfulness allows the meditator to step out of the cycle of thinking and over time, we learn to meet the ups and downs of life with non-attachment, and more a peaceful state.

So often, we focus on the negative in our lives, and our lives seem to become more and more negative.

One way of *nurturing positivity*, is to become mindful of the positive experiences as we experience them.

Think of a time when you felt that things were going brilliantly, and circumstances felt right.

You were in the flow and you may have felt in a state of grace. Where were you? Who else was there?

Reflect on this time, and go deeper into the memory. Let the feeling grow and observe how you are feeling, in yourself, in your face, in your body?

What do you feel like doing? What thoughts are you having?

You may find you want to talk to someone and share.

You will feel lighter, taller, happier. You will radiate laughter and joy.

Just like negative emotions, positive emotions are embodied and are just waiting to be acknowledged and felt.

Another thing you can do, is just stop.

Sit in the quiet, be still and breathe.

Forget about what is going on around you and give yourself the space, you need to breathe *you*.

Slowly, deeply, quietly, patiently.

Come back to you and remember *you*.

Spiritual practice offers us the opportunity to write and alternative narrative for our lives. One that fosters wellness and happiness.

In this way, spiritual practice is quite radical, and individual to each of us.

Chakras

7 Colours, 7 Chakras, 7 Belief Systems

777 — relates to the balance and rhythm of our physical being. The 7 steps to you, guide you to being, *Your Beautiful Rainbow*.

The colours of the rainbow;

red, orange, yellow, green, blue, indigo, violet are associated with the seven chakra colours.

The energy centres of our being.

> *A wound not fully felt consumes from inside. We must run very hard if we want to stay one step ahead of the pain.* – Oriah Mountain Dreamer

What Is a Chakra?

Borrowing from Hinduism, the 7 chakras, (pronounced cha-kra, ch as in church), dates back to 1500 BC and literally means, 'wheel.' They symbolize a circle, or the eternal. It is also a metaphor of the sun. More importantly chakras are meant to spin. We are beings that need to be in motion, to keep progressing through life.

Chakras are used to connect to the non-physical aspect of ourselves, which is thought to be separate from the physical self. Buddhists believe the chakra and its 'circle' symbolizes rebirth.

There's more and more evidence backing up these timeless beliefs. Modern physiology confirms these 7 chakras correspond exactly to the 7 main nerve ganglia which emanate from the spinal column.

A chakra is a centre of energy. The work chakra means disk. It is where we store our programming, the beliefs we have taken on, from the moment of our birth, and previous lifetimes.

We have 7 main energy centres that sit in the main core of our body. When they are spinning freely and brightly, we are living in respect and honour of our being. When they are sluggish and dull, we are allowing our fear to guide us, causing holes in our aura. Our emotional aspect of our self.

Our aura is the non-visible field that surrounds our body. Each chakra has its own vibrational frequency and is a specific colour; like a rainbow.

Each chakra is associated with our emotional self and our belief system; which corresponds in our physical health and wellbeing.

Holes in our aura develop when one or more of our energy centres is thrown off balance by a blockage in our emotional self, this then causes a disturbance in our physical body, manifesting in a physical sickness or disease.

As we live through our lives, we lose sight of our emotions, looking outside of our energy field to give us what we think we need, never feeling enough or complete. Often living in a place of loneliness.

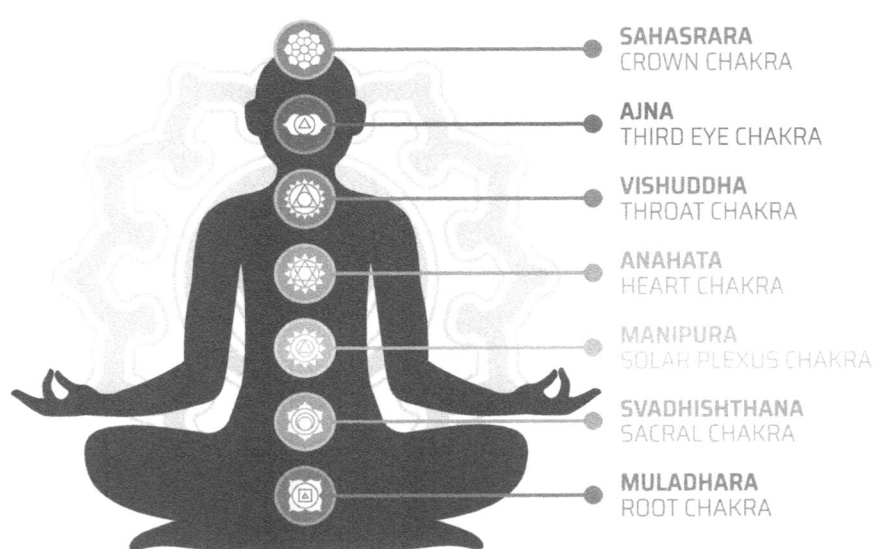

Chakras & Numbers 1 – 7

Root–Red   being in our own energy with ourselves
Sacral–Orange   being in our relationship with ourselves
Solar Plexus–Yellow being in our creation of ourselves
Heart–Green   being in our connection with ourselves
Throat–Blue   being in our awareness of ourselves
Third Eye–Indigo   being in our *knowing* of ourselves
Crown–Violet   being in our alignment of ourselves.

The chakra is impacted by life experiences. It's as if our experiences imprint energetic patterns into the chakras, and influence the way they work.

Negative experiences have a particularly strong impact as they often result in raising defenses, translating in suppression or contraction of the energy flowing through our chakras.

We carry negative emotions within our being, painful childhood memories, grief, loss of a loved one, regrets, marriage breakup, sexual abuse or violation.

We have all suffered or been exposed to rejection, denial, failure, hardship, and guilt to some degree.

We must allow ourselves to feel. Our resistance to feeling any negative emotion has to manifest in some way in our being. Without the correct foundation and support we harbour resentment, anger, confusion and low energy. Overtime our body will breakdown, physically.

This is what happens when we talk about a chakra blockage. Even though imbalances are often described in terms of 'closed', or 'blocked' chakra, it is more accurate to use the images of diminution or increase energy flow.

When a chakra is 'blocked', it means that the amount and quality of energy it produces, and flows through, is highly reduced.

Chakra healing aims at supporting a balanced flow of energy throughout the whole body, or on specific parts of the body.

Stop – make time for you

Breathe – rhythmic breaths

Be – grounded, in your awareness

Ask – 'what do I want to know?'

Listen – from within

Allow – your soul to speak

Write – down what you are feeling

Red
Root Chakra – Self Love

The Root Chakra sits at the base of our spine and is our foundation of self-love. Our support of who we are. The associated belief is one of self-love. We must feel our foundation of love to the root of our being, to grow from within.

The foundation of self-love must be strong to support all aspects of our self, otherwise our structure will crumble and fall.

This is the centre of self, standing in our power and flow of our love.

Imbalances in this chakra may manifest as:
- ~ problems with our legs and circulation.
- ~ amputations
- ~ deep vein thrombosis
- ~ fungal and nail infections
- ~ bunions
- ~ cold feet
- ~ spurs
- ~ oedema
- ~ varicose veins
- ~ leg ulcers
- ~ leg cramps
- ~ falling over.

Imbalance of this chakra is reflective of our own ability to stand strong in our love of our self, and move forward in who we are.

Feel your way to your Root Chakra

It is a process. Begin at your leisure. Turn the television off. Turn the radio off.

Put on some soft music, or just have some quiet time.

Meditation is not just about sitting quietly in a yoga position.

The definition of meditation is the, *Continued or extended thought, contemplation, reflection.*

You can meditate at any time, when you have a few minutes to yourself; washing the dishes, folding the washing, vacuuming, in the shower, on the toilet, even in the car.

Anytime, you are in the, *zone*. Just allow yourself to be with you and listen to you. Even if it is just for a few minutes.

If you can, go outside and just stand and breathe.

I am often going about my daily life and I will hear a dog bark, or a bird sing, or a song and I will realise the significance of something being brought to my awareness, or confirmation of what I have been thinking, or asking unconsciously.

Because I am asking my soul, there is no judgement or agenda, as we are connected to all things, at every moment. The universe will respond in different ways, always.

If I am feeling unsettled, or want an answer, I will go for a walk, talk out loud, ask, 'Help me, show me, tell me,' And a bird will sing or a gecko will chirp. I feel the support of the universe. In this space of being, the answers do come.

We just have to trust and know that when we ask, we receive.

Allow

Look in the mirror every morning and say, 'I love you.'

Feel it within you.

If you feel emotions come up, allow it.

Stop
Drink a glass of water.
Sit or stand in a quiet space.
Close your eyes.

Breathe
Put your left hand over your chest, and your right hand over your root chakra—Just at the front of the base of your spine.

Breathe deeply; breathe in to the count of 5, pause, and say to affirmation; *'I feel my love within me.'*

Breathe out to the count of 7.

Repeat 7 times.

Feel
Feel your balance and a sense of peace within.

See
Visualise the colour red, flowing through your root chakra.

Ask
Ask yourself a question, anything

Listen
Allow yourself to feel, you may get an answer from within, or you may hear a gecko, or a bird chirp, a dog bark, or a car beep.

Write
Before you go to sleep write down how you have been feeling. Have you been feeling upset, angry, frustrated, blessed, grateful, or anything that has come to your attention.

Write down 7 things you are grateful for.

Write down a question, you would like an answer to.

Let your soul speak, as you sleep. You will wake up, with clarity and an answer.

If you feel any emotions, come up, allow it and surrender.

You may feel a sense of helplessness, or anxiousness. You may cry. Feel out of control. It is just the shift in your energy. The letting go of suppressed emotions. Remember to breathe.

Orange
Sacral Chakra – Self Worth

The sacral chakra sits just below our navel and is our centre of our gender, male or female. The associated belief is one of self-worth. Our centre of worthiness, standing in our true worth as male or female. To feel our own worthiness of what we are, from within. Otherwise, we cannot create fully in our masculine or feminine energy causing stagnation in the reproduction of our true selves. Keeping us in the pattern of giving ourselves away to others, and not feeling our worth.

This is the centre of our support system, and flow of our own feminine and masculine energy.

Imbalances in this chakra may manifest as:
- ~ problems with elimination of toxic waste from our body.
- ~ problems with the urinary system and bladder
- ~ reproductive problems
- ~ prostatic problems
- ~ endometriosis
- ~ menorrhagia
- ~ period problems
- ~ problems with conceiving
- ~ irritable bowel
- ~ flatulence
- ~ haemorrhoids

- bowel cancer
- constipation
- diarrhoea
- lower back problems.

Urinary tract infections signify, being 'pissed off.'

Incontinence, not being in our own power.

Imbalance of this chakra is reflective of the blocking of our emotions, holding on to fear and not flowing freely in support of our worthiness in who we are.

Feel your way to your Sacral Chakra:

It is a process. Begin at your leisure. Turn the television off. Turn the radio off.

Put on some soft music, or just have some quiet time.

Meditation is not just about sitting quietly in a yoga position.

The definition of meditation is the, *Continued or extended thought, contemplation, reflection.*

You can meditate at any time, when you have a few minutes to yourself, washing the dishes, folding the washing, vacuuming, in the shower, on the toilet, even in the car.

Anytime, you are in the, *zone*. Just allow yourself to be with you and listen to you. Even if it is just for a few minutes.

If you can, go outside and just stand and breathe.

I am often going about my daily life and I will hear a dog bark, or a bird sing, or a song and I will realise the significance of something being brought to my awareness, or confirmation of what I have been thinking, or asking unconsciously.

Because I am asking my soul, there is no judgement or agenda as we are connected to all things, at every moment. The universe will respond in different ways, always.

If I am feeling unsettled, or want an answer, I will go for a walk, talk out loud, ask, 'Help me, show me, tell me,' And a bird will sing or a gecko will chirp.

I feel the support of the universe. In this space of being, the answers do come.

We just have to trust and know that when we ask, we receive.

Allow

Look in the mirror every morning and say, 'I love you.'

Feel it within you.

If you feel emotions come up, allow it.

Stop

Drink a glass of water.
Sit or stand in a quiet space.
Close your eyes.

Breathe

Put your left hand over your chest, and your right hand over your sacral chakra.

Breathe deeply; breathe in to the count of 5, pause, and say to affirmation; *'I feel my worth within me.'*

Breathe out to the count of 7.
Repeat 7 times.

Feel

Feel your balance and a sense of peace within.

See

Visualise the colour orange, flowing through your sacral chakra.

Ask

Ask yourself a question, anything

Listen

Allow yourself to feel, you may get an answer from within, or you may hear a gecko, or a bird chirp, a dog bark, or a car beep.

Write

Before you go to sleep write down how you have been feeling. Have you been feeling upset, angry, frustrated, blessed, grateful, or anything that has come to your attention.

Write down 7 things you are grateful for.

Write down a question, you would like an answer to.

Let your soul speak, as you sleep. You will wake up, with clarity and an answer.

If you feel any emotions, come up, allow it and surrender.

You may feel a sense of helplessness, or anxiousness. You may cry. Feel out of control. It is just the shift in your energy. The letting go of suppressed emotions. Remember to breathe.

Yellow
Solar Plexus Chakra – Self Value

The solar plexus chakra sits just above our navel and is the centre of our emotions, our joy and happiness. The associated belief is self-value.

Our emotional, happiness centre. Where our sun shines. We have to feel our emotions on every level and shine from within. Our centre to nurture ourselves with goodness.

Imbalances in this chakra may manifest as:
- ~ problems with extended abdomen
- ~ gastritis
- ~ stomach ulcers
- ~ stomach aches
- ~ indigestion
- ~ digestive issues
- ~ nausea
- ~ vomiting
- ~ diabetes
- ~ liver problems
- ~ pancreatitis.

Lack of joy, or the presence of anger, can be the cause of problems in this area.

Diabetes occurs, when there is no joy from within, and the body is craving the sweetness, it has lost the ability to feel.

The blocking of your flow to process your anger, to one of value of you.

The shutting down of your emotional self.

It represents your inability to take responsibility to digest you, and remember how to feel your value.

Many men and women who have an extended abdomen, are deflecting their inability to feel their own emotions; or don't want to feel.

As they have shut down their emotional aspect to protect themselves from being *hurt,* denying themselves how to feel their value.

Feel your way to your Solar Plexus Chakra:

It is a process. Begin at your leisure. Turn the television off. Turn the radio off.

Put on some soft music, or just have some quiet time.

Meditation is not just about sitting quietly in a yoga position.

The definition of meditation is the, *Continued or extended thought, contemplation, reflection.*

You can meditate at any time, when you have a few minutes to yourself, washing the dishes, folding the washing, vacuuming, in the shower, on the toilet, even in the car.

Anytime, you are in the, *zone*. Just allow yourself to be with you and listen to you. Even if it is just for a few minutes.

If you can, go outside and just stand and breathe.

I am often going about my daily life and I will hear a dog bark, or a bird sing, or a song and I will realise the significance of something being brought to my awareness, or confirmation of what I have been thinking, or asking unconsciously.

Because I am asking my soul, there is no judgement or agenda as we are connected to all things, at every moment. The universe will respond in different ways, always.

If I am feeling unsettled, or want an answer, I will go for a walk, talk out loud, ask, 'Help me, show me, tell me,' And a bird will sing or a gecko will chirp.

I feel the support of the universe. In this space of being, the answers do come.

We just have to trust and know that when we ask, we receive.

Allow

Look in the mirror every morning and say, 'I love you.'

Feel it within you.

If you feel emotions come up, allow it.

Stop
Drink a glass of water.
Sit or stand in a quiet space.
Close your eyes.

Breathe
Put your left hand over your chest, and your right hand over your solar plexus chakra.

Breathe deeply; breathe in to the count of 5, pause, and say to affirmation; *'I feel my value within me'*

Breathe out to the count of 7.

Repeat 7 times.

Feel
Feel your balance and a sense of peace within.

See
Visualise the colour yellow, flowing through your solar plexus chakra.

Ask
Ask yourself a question, anything

Listen
Allow yourself to feel, you may get an answer from within, or you may hear a gecko, or a bird chirp, a dog bark, or a car beep.

Write
Before you go to sleep write down how you have been feeling. Have you been feeling upset, angry, frustrated, blessed, grateful, or anything that has come to your attention.

Write down 7 things you are grateful for.

Write down a question, you would like an answer to.

Let your soul speak, as you sleep. You will wake up, with

clarity and an answer.

If you feel any emotions, come up, allow it and surrender.

You may feel a sense of helplessness, or anxiousness. You may cry. Feel out of control. It is just the shift in your energy. The letting go of suppressed emotions. Remember to breathe.

Green
Heart Chakra – Self Acceptance

The heart chakra sits in our mid chest, and is the centre of acceptance of our ability to love ourselves, and love others. The associated belief is one of self-acceptance. When we are unable to accept, and receive our love, heart problems may occur. It is the centre where our blood flows around our body. Our life-line.

Imbalances in this chakra may manifest as:
- problems with heart and lungs
- heart attacks
- blocked arteries
- need for a pacemaker
- angina
- chest infections
- bronchitis
- pneumonia
- asthma
- pulmonary oedema
- chronic obstructive airway disease
- hypertension
- hypotension
- breast cancer.

Often, we live in the need to be accepted by another, living in abandonment of our own needs. If we are not living in acceptance of our flow, allowing ourselves to breathe for us. Feel our own nurturing, what we need for our self, our circulation system will start to fail.

Chest problems reflect our grief, our loss of ourselves.

Heart problems reflect our inability to accept or receive our self-love.

Breast problems reflect our inability to nurture ourselves.

We have to remember to breathe in our goodness of our self.

Feel your way to your Heart Chakra:

It is a process. Begin at your leisure. Turn the television off. Turn the radio off.

Put on some soft music, or just have some quiet time.

Meditation is not just about sitting quietly in a yoga position.

The definition of meditation is the, *Continued or extended thought, contemplation, reflection.*

You can meditate at any time, when you have a few minutes to yourself, washing the dishes, folding the washing, vacuuming, in the shower, on the toilet, even in the car.

Anytime, you are in the, *zone*. Just allow yourself to be with you and listen to you. Even if it is just for a few minutes.

If you can, go outside and just stand and breathe.

I am often going about my daily life and I will hear a dog bark, or a bird sing, or a song and I will realise the significance of something being brought to my awareness, or confirmation of what I have been thinking, or asking unconsciously.

Because I am asking my soul, there is no judgement or agenda as we are connected to all things, at every moment. The universe will respond in different ways, always.

If I am feeling unsettled, or want an answer, I will go for a walk, talk out loud, ask, 'Help me, show me, tell me,' And a bird will sing or a gecko will chirp.

I feel the support of the universe. In this space of being, the answers do come.

We just have to trust and know that when we ask, we receive.

Allow

Look in the mirror every morning and say, 'I love you.'

Feel it within you.

If you feel emotions come up, allow it.

Stop
Drink a glass of water.
Sit or stand in a quiet space.
Close your eyes.

Breathe
Put your left hand over your chest, and your right hand over your heart chakra.

Breathe deeply; breathe in to the count of 5, pause, and say to affirmation; *'I feel my acceptance within me'*

Breathe out to the count of 7.

Repeat 7 times.

Feel
Feel your balance and a sense of peace within.

See
Visualise the colour green, flowing through your heart chakra.

Ask
Ask yourself a question, anything

Listen
Allow yourself to feel, you may get an answer from within, or you may hear a gecko, or a bird chirp, a dog bark, or a car beep.

Write
Before you go to sleep write down how you have been feeling. Have you been feeling upset, angry, frustrated, blessed, grateful, or anything that has come to your attention.

Write down 7 things you are grateful for.

Write down a question, you would like an answer to.

Let your soul speak, as you sleep. You will wake up, with clarity and an answer.

If you feel any emotions, come up, allow it and surrender.

You may feel a sense of helplessness, or anxiousness. You may cry. Feel out of control. It is just the shift in your energy. The letting go of suppressed emotions. Remember to breathe.

Blue
Throat Chakra – Self Belief

The throat chakra sits in our throat and is the centre of our communication with ourselves and others. To feel our adequacy to speak our truth. The associated belief is one of self-belief. It is the bridge, connecting our heads to our hearts. Our way of communicating our truth, honesty and acknowledgement, speaking from our heart space. Knowing we are adequate.

When we feel unable to speak up and the throat chakra is blocked, not believing ourselves worthy to say what needs to be said, we may experience sore throats, neck pain, or laryngitis.

Imbalances in this chakra may manifest as:
- ~ problems with tonsilitis
- ~ sore throats
- ~ quinsy
- ~ coughs
- ~ mouth ulcers
- ~ dry mouth
- ~ throat cancer
- ~ thyroid problems
- ~ toothache
- ~ abscesses.

So often, we do not acknowledge or voice ourselves freely, or trust ourselves to speak our truth. Allowing our ego to override our fears, causing blockages and stagnation of energy.

Feeling inadequate and lacking confidence in our ability to be in our power.

Feel your way to your Throat Chakra:

It is a process. Begin at your leisure. Turn the television off. Turn the radio off.

Put on some soft music, or just have some quiet time.

Meditation is not just about sitting quietly in a yoga position.

The definition of meditation is the, *Continued or extended thought, contemplation, reflection.*

You can meditate at any time, when you have a few minutes to yourself, washing the dishes, folding the washing, vacuuming, in the shower, on the toilet, even in the car.

Anytime, you are in the, *zone*. Just allow yourself to be with you and listen to you. Even if it is just for a few minutes.

If you can, go outside and just stand and breathe.

I am often going about my daily life and I will hear a dog bark, or a bird sing, or a song and I will realise the significance of something being brought to my awareness, or confirmation of what I have been thinking, or asking unconsciously.

Because I am asking my soul, there is no judgement or agenda as we are connected to all things, at every moment. The universe will respond in different ways, always.

If I am feeling unsettled, or want an answer, I will go for a walk, talk out loud, ask, 'Help me, show me, tell me,' And a bird will sing or a gecko will chirp.

I feel the support of the universe. In this space of being, the answers do come.

We just have to trust and know that when we ask, we receive.

Allow

Look in the mirror every morning and say, 'I love you.'

Feel it within you.

If you feel emotions come up, allow it.

Stop
> Drink a glass of water.
> Sit or stand in a quiet space.
> Close your eyes.

Breathe
> Put your left hand over your chest, and your right hand over your throat chakra.
> Breathe deeply; breathe in to the count of 5, pause, and say to affirmation; *'I feel my belief within me'*
> Breathe out to the count of 7.
> Repeat 7 times.

Feel
> Feel your balance and a sense of peace within.

See
> Visualise the colour blue, flowing through your throat chakra.

Ask
> Ask yourself a question, anything

Listen
> Allow yourself to feel, you may get an answer from within, or you may hear a gecko, or a bird chirp, a dog bark, or a car beep.

Write
> Before you go to sleep write down how you have been feeling. Have you been feeling upset, angry, frustrated, blessed, grateful, or anything that has come to your attention.
> Write down 7 things you are grateful for.
> Write down a question, you would like an answer to.
> Let your soul speak, as you sleep. You will wake up, with clarity and an answer.

If you feel any emotions, come up, allow it and surrender.

You may feel a sense of helplessness, or anxiousness. You may cry. Feel out of control. It is just the shift in your energy. The letting go of suppressed emotions. Remember to breathe.

Indigo
Third Eye Chakra – Self Trust

The third eye chakra sits in between our eyes, mid brow and is the centre of our intuition and inner *knowing*. The associated belief is one of self-trust.

At the end of the day, no one knows us better than our self. We must trust, listen and follow our inner *knowing*, our voice within.

Imbalances of this chakra may manifest as:
- problems with headaches
- eye problems
- glaucoma
- cataracts
- poor eyesight
- dry eyes
- styes
- hearing problems
- blocked ears
- earache
- ringing in the ears
- dizziness
- Not seeing our truth or trusting in our *knowing*.

If we cannot see who we are, or see where we are going, we may develop eye sight issues.

If we are not prepared to listen to our inner voice, or listen to what we don't want to hear, we may develop ear problems.

Feel your way to your Third Eye Chakra:

It is a process. Begin at your leisure. Turn the television off. Turn the radio off.

Put on some soft music, or just have some quiet time.

Meditation is not just about sitting quietly in a yoga position.

The definition of meditation is the, *Continued or extended thought, contemplation, reflection.*

You can meditate at any time, when you have a few minutes to yourself, washing the dishes, folding the washing, vacuuming, in the shower, on the toilet, even in the car.

Anytime, you are in the, *zone*. Just allow yourself to be with you and listen to you. Even if it is just for a few minutes.

If you can, go outside and just stand and breathe.

I am often going about my daily life and I will hear a dog bark, or a bird sing, or a song and I will realise the significance of something being brought to my awareness, or confirmation of what I have been thinking, or asking unconsciously.

Because I am asking my soul, there is no judgement or agenda as we are connected to all things, at every moment. The universe will respond in different ways, always.

If I am feeling unsettled, or want an answer, I will go for a walk, talk out loud, ask, 'Help me, show me, tell me,' And a bird will sing or a gecko will chirp.

I feel the support of the universe. In this space of being, the answers do come.

We just have to trust and know that when we ask, we receive.

Allow

Look in the mirror every morning and say, 'I love you.'
Feel it within you.
If you feel emotions come up, allow it.

Stop

Drink a glass of water.
Sit or stand in a quiet space.
Close your eyes.

Breathe

Put your left hand over your heart, and your right hand over your third eye chakra.

Breathe deeply; breathe in to the count of 5, pause, and say to affirmation; *'I feel my trust within me'*

Breathe out to the count of 7.
Repeat 7 times.

Feel

Feel your balance and a sense of peace within.

See

Visualise the colour indigo, flowing through your third eye chakra.

Ask

Ask yourself a question, anything

Listen

Allow yourself to feel, you may get an answer from within, or you may hear a gecko, or a bird chirp, a dog bark, or a car beep.

Write

Before you go to sleep write down how you have been feeling. Have you been feeling upset, angry, frustrated, blessed, grateful, or anything that has come to your attention.

Write down 7 things you are grateful for.

Write down a question, you would like an answer to.

Let your soul speak, as you sleep. You will wake up, with clarity and an answer.

If you feel any emotions, come up, allow it and surrender.

You may feel a sense of helplessness, or anxiousness. You may cry. Feel out of control. It is just the shift in your energy. The letting go of suppressed emotions. Remember to breathe.

Violet
Crown Chakra – Self Faith

The crown chakra sits in the middle of the top of our head and is the centre of our connection to our higher self. The associated belief is one of self-faith.

Our centre of our connection to the higher dimension of the universe, where we are fully supported for who we are unconditionally. We just have to live in support and love of our self; Trusting the grounding of our love and our connection to the higher realm of consciousness.

Imbalances in this chakra may manifest as:
- ~ problems with headaches
- ~ brain injuries
- ~ aneurysms
- ~ blood clots
- ~ brain tumours
- ~ multiple sclerosis
- ~ motor neurone disease
- ~ parkinson's diseas
- ~ dementia
- ~ epilepsy
- ~ bumps to the head.

If we live in denial of our connection and fear of 'something else', that we cannot see; we may develop brain problems.

Having operations, taking the 'magic pill' may treat the symptoms, but will not always shift the emotional factor.

People who get constant headaches or migraines may not be living in awareness of their connection to all things. They may not have faith in themselves to be anything else than what they see.

Feel your way to your Crown Chakra:

It is a process. Begin at your leisure. Turn the television off. Turn the radio off.

Put on some soft music, or just have some quiet time.

Meditation is not just about sitting quietly in a yoga position.

The definition of meditation is the, *Continued or extended thought, contemplation, reflection.*

You can meditate at any time, when you have a few minutes to yourself, washing the dishes, folding the washing, vacuuming, in the shower, on the toilet, even in the car.

Anytime, you are in the, *zone*. Just allow yourself to be with you and listen to you. Even if it is just for a few minutes.

If you can, go outside and just stand and breathe.

I am often going about my daily life and I will hear a dog bark, or a bird sing, or a song and I will realise the significance of something being brought to my awareness, or confirmation of what I have been thinking, or asking unconsciously.

Because I am asking my soul, there is no judgement or agenda as we are connected to all things, at every moment. The universe will respond in different ways, always.

If I am feeling unsettled, or want an answer, I will go for a walk, talk out loud, ask, 'Help me, show me, tell me,' And a bird will sing or a gecko will chirp.

I feel the support of the universe. In this space of being, the answers do come.

We just have to trust and know that when we ask, we receive.

Allow
Look in the mirror every morning and say, 'I love you.'
Feel it within you.
If you feel emotions come up, allow it.

Stop
Drink a glass of water.
Sit or stand in a quiet space.
Close your eyes.

Breathe
Put your left hand over your heart, and your right hand over your third crown chakra.

Breathe deeply; breathe in to the count of 5, pause, and say to affirmation; *'I feel my faith within me'*

Breathe out to the count of 7.

Repeat 7 times.

Feel
Feel your balance and a sense of peace within.

See
Visualise the colour violet, flowing through your crown chakra.

Ask
Ask yourself a question, anything

Listen
Allow yourself to feel, you may get an answer from within, or you may hear a gecko, or a bird chirp, a dog bark, or a car beep.

Write
Before you go to sleep write down how you have been feeling. Have you been feeling upset, angry, frustrated, blessed, grateful, or anything that has come to your attention.

Write down 7 things you are grateful for.

Write down a question, you would like an answer to.

Let your soul speak, as you sleep. You will wake up, with clarity and an answer.

If you feel any emotions, come up, allow it and surrender.

You may feel a sense of helplessness, or anxiousness. You may cry. Feel out of control. It is just the shift in your energy. The letting go of suppressed emotions. Remember to breathe.

Case Studies

The following are actual examples of people's personal conditions.

Our body is our temple and our greatest messenger. It will never do us wrong, although we may not want to take on board what it is telling us.

When we are sick or unwell, stop, take time to sit and reflect.

Where is the discomfort in your body? Is it associated with your left or right side? How does it make you feel? What is the emotion coming up, do you feel helpless, hopeless, pathetic, frustrated, angry?

Breathe into the pain or discomfort, give it the attention it is asking for. It wants to be acknowledged. Write down how you are feeling.

Don't forget all the answers are within you. You know, listen and trust you.

Case Study One

A woman who had been adopted. She suffered from high blood pressure, in her inability to accept her love of herself. She is blocking her ability to open to her heart, as she does not want to take responsibility of feeling the abandonment from her mother. And in reflection is abandoning herself. She also suffered from anaphylaxis, the collapse of the body due to an allergic reaction to something; unable to digest and receive herself.

She has also been bitten by a whitetail spider on her left foot; causing her to lose her toenails and have sores on both feet. Reflecting her inability to flow in her feminine power stand in her own self-love; and open her heart to herself.

Case Study Two

A woman had a stiff right side of her neck. The right side is your male, physical side. She is carrying a burden, the responsibility of others.

She is also allowing a certain male in her life to hook into her power subconsciously. She is not allowing herself to feel her power, or be in her flow as a woman; being out of balance and not respecting her emotional needs.

As she recognized the message, the pain in her neck went. It got the attention it was looking for. She then developed pain in her left hand. As the burden, had left her body, it gave room for her spiritual (left) side to wake up. She can now respect the flow of her being and feel her feminine energy.

Case Study Three

A young man had an abscess between his eyes, the second one in 6 months. The space between his eyes is his third eye. His *knowing*, his intuition. He was not listening to his inner voice. He was blocking it. That he acknowledged when I discussed this with him, due to a certain situation in his life.

There is something he has to acknowledge to open up to his *knowing*. To live in respect of his power. As the abscess is oozing, it is signifying he is not respecting or trusting his inner *knowing* and is giving away his power to others.

Case Study Four

A young student had dermatitis on her 3rd finger of her right hand, and a painful left shin. She had just broken up with her boyfriend of 6 years.

Her fingers are all about feeling her way, by herself; and her legs are about moving forward. The message for her was, it is ok for her to be herself without her boyfriend. To trust herself to let go the connection to him, the irritation in her fingers, her emotional doubt of herself. Not realising her worth as a woman.

It is ok for her to feel her way. The pain in her left leg was her blocking her ability to step forward in her power and allowing to trust her ability to take responsibility for herself.

Case Study Five

A young staff member was feeling sick from anxiety and was feeling exhausted. She could find no reason why.

As she breathed, the emotion came up and the tears started to flow. As the tears flowed, the anxiety subsided, she stopped feeling sick.

The emotion was acknowledged.

Case Study Six

A woman had problems with her right knee. This is her male, physical side. She is not standing in her power and is allowing a male to feed her feeling of not being enough.

Shortly after she had two flat tyres on the left side of the car. The car is her vehicle to carry her forward. She is scared to feel herself and support herself emotionally. Move in the flow of her feminine power.

Thank you, thank you, thank you,
thank you to me.
For all who I am and all that I be.
I am unique and one of a kind,
in acceptance of my body and of my mind.
I live my life in respect of me,
with no excuses of what I *should* be.
I do my best of that I can say,
at home, at work and also at play.
I live in daily support of me
and take on being my responsibility.
I am so wonderful, loving and caring.
For me to acknowledge is so daring.
I am of worthy and value,
of that I can see.
I am so grateful to be me.
I believe in myself and the choices I make,
for these are the ones I am meant to take.
For all that I am and all that I be,
all that matters at the end of the day is me.

Karen Houston

About The Author

I am Karen and I am Pixie. I was born Karen Anne Houston.

Karen is what I am known as by my family. Pixie is what my friends call me. Both names are aspects of me and support me in who I am.

All my life, I have had a *knowing* of something else. I do not believe this is it, we are born, we grow up, we die. There is a greater purpose for all. Although my life has been content in many ways, I have always felt something was missing. I had a yearning but did not fully understand what was missing, or what I was yearning for. Often told as a child, 'to get my head out of the clouds and put my feet on the ground.'

When I was a little girl, I used to lie in my bed at night and feel my mouth was small like a bird and my head was the size of the room. It was a strange, but familiar, and comforting feeling. I felt connected and supported to myself and all things. I was feeling my expansion of my emotional body, my non-physical aspect of myself.

As I grew the feeling went away and did not return until 2001, 35 years later. The message, I was reconnecting to all aspects of myself and my soul was telling me to trust and follow my heart, believe in my ability to respect my journey.

In my innocence as a child, I asked to become a nurse; to travel and live in Australia, to have 3 children, two boys and a girl. All that I asked for has manifested in every way. I also asked to be stripped of my human reality, to come back to me. Little did I know what I was asking for.

I was married for 25 years, have 3 beautiful children and life was good. A few years ago, I began to feel suffocated and confused. I left my marriage. Nothing had happened to make me leave. I just felt I couldn't breathe. My soul was telling me it was time to face myself on every level. I left, with literally the clothes on my back.

I lost my home, all my family and friends turned their backs on me. I was on my own. I asked for this. I had to stop living the illusion and feel myself, face myself, allow myself to let all my suppressed emotions come to the surface to be acknowledged.

I did a lot of reflection, listening. I asked for direction. I felt my anger and my abandonment of myself. At times, it was challenging, I wanted to give up. It was daunting. But I am truly grateful for the opportunity I have had to come back to me.

Prior to leaving, I was working long hours about an hour from where I live. My car gave up the ghost and had to be sold for parts. Our car is our vehicle which takes us from A to B. Our body is our vehicle that carries us through our life. Our car is our reflection of ourselves. When my car stopped, it was telling me to stop and change direction. At the time, I didn't listen. I got a new car and kept going. One night driving home, the radiator hose disconnected and the radiator ran dry. A reflection, I was draining myself of everything, physically and emotionally. I had to stop. So, I listened. I left my job which was what had been holding the illusion together, and I realised that there was no support for me. I was allowing myself to be led by others needs and not my own. I left everything and everyone behind.

One night sometime later, someone hit my car on the left side and it was written off. Another message from the universe. Although I had left, I was not giving myself, the respect of my emotional needs as a woman.

I had to get a new car. I bought a blue car without realising the significance at the time. Blue is the colour of flow, belief, acknowledgement and adequacy. Belief in me. That is all I had. It is as if, I had prepared myself subconsciously. I had no control. I just had to trust in me.

We all have a choice, to hide, or to be vulnerable to ourselves.

I have been writing this book on my computer and in my head, for many years. I have also been journalling many things about life and love. I have always had an understanding that our physical bodies reflect the emotions that we carry in our energy field.

I am very organised, and having lived a decluttered life, have assisted others along the way. The philosophy being, having the correct foundation from which to live, be and grow. When there is clutter, there is confusion. When there is no clutter, there is clarity.

Our conditioning is our clutter. Often people create physical clutter subconsciously to try to fill a void that they are lacking in themselves. Physical clutter is an avoidance of emotional clutter, causing stagnant energy, keeping people from facing their true selves.

When there is love, there is no need to fill our life up with stuff that no longer serves us. Physically, the material goods, the need to buy. Emotionally, the abuse, abandonment, denial, betrayal of our self.

I have been a nurse for many years, mainly in aged care. I have met many wonderful people with amazing life stories. But I can't help wondering about life. I look at these people and others, care for their pain and suffering and thinking life doesn't have to be like this. Every ailment, sickness, disease or situation is a blockage in our emotional body that manifests in our physical reality. A cause and effect. We can heal ourselves and be free of pain and suffering. We just have to be in awareness and respect of our emotional body.

I have had my own ailments to contend with over the years, signifying my emotional aspects of myself that I have denied. Where I have followed what is expected of me by others and have tried to fit into society, on another's terms.

A few years ago, I was running myself ragged in a well-paid position, as an aged care funding manager. On one level, I could justify it, working Monday to Friday, with flexible hours. But I was struggling with the job itself on principle and morally. It went against my belief system. The universe stopped me, literally by throwing me off a stool. I hurt my lower back and couldn't work for 6 months. My lower back is my support system. The message was about supporting and listening to me and not a system that was corrupt and I didn't believe in.

My first son was born in Australia. We then moved back to Scotland for a few years. My second son was born. After he was born, I developed shingles, a symptom of low immunity and I also developed pleurisy, the sticking of my lungs. I was not breathing for me. I was living my life by the expectations of others.

As a child, I was plagued with tonsillitis and earache. Tonsils reflect my inability to speak my truth and my living in fear of being heard. Earache represents me not wanting to listen to what is going on around me, and not being able to change it. Not allowing myself to listen to my *knowing* due to fear. Having them removed, does not shift the belief. The emotion has to be felt.

As a teenager, I had anorexia. Anorexia is about not having any acceptance of myself. I thought I could control my unacceptance, by controlling what I ate.

So, when I write, you only belong to yourself. I know. We are responsible for ourselves and no one else. As we live our journey of discovery of our truth; one by one, we help others to do the same. We naturally attract that support into our lives, connecting to the oneness of all that is.

I now invite you to open the door to your awareness of your whole self and take yourself on this journey from within.

Karen

Source references

http://www.chakras.info/

http://www.enlightenedfeelings.com/body.html#emotions chart

http://www.selfgrowth.com/articles/two_energies_one_body.html

http://www.carliniinstitute.com/the_ego_and_the_soul

https://en.wikipedia.org/wiki/Harry_Harlow

https://theknowing1.wordpress.com/panacea/?blogsub=confirming#blog_ subscription-3

http://sqi.co/ego-and-soul/ http://www.simplypsychology.org/maslow.html https://en.m.wikipedia.org/wiki/Chakra